Kitchen & Bath Systems

Mechanical ◆ Electrical ◆ Plumbing

Jerry Germer

NKBA
The Finest Professionals in the Kitchen & Bath Industry
National Kitchen & Bath Association℠

Professional Resource Library

About The National Kitchen & Bath Association

As the only non-profit trade association dedicated exclusively to the kitchen and bath industry, the National Kitchen & Bath Association (NKBA) is the leading source of information and education for all professionals in the field.

NKBA's mission is to enhance member success and excellence by promoting professionalism and ethical business practices, and by providing leadership and direction for the kitchen and bath industry.

A non-profit trade association with more than 25,000 members in North America and overseas, it has provided valuable resources for industry professionals for more than forty years. Its members are the finest professionals in the kitchen and bath industry.

NKBA has pioneered innovative industry research, developed effective business management tools, and set groundbreaking standards for safe, functional and comfortable design of kitchens and baths.

NKBA provides a unique, one-stop resource for professional reference materials, seminars and workshops, distance learning opportunities, marketing assistance, design competitions, consumer referrals, job and internship opportunities and opportunities for volunteer leadership activities.

Recognized as the kitchen and bath industry's education and information leader, NKBA provides development opportunities and continuing education for all levels of professionals. More than 100 courses, as well as a certification program with three internationally recognized levels, help kitchen and bath professionals raise the bar for excellence.

For students entering the industry, NKBA offers Supported and Endorsed Programs, which provide NKBA-approved curriculum at more than 47 learning institutions throughout North America.

NKBA helps members and other industry professionals stay on the cutting-edge of an ever-changing field through the Association's Kitchen/Bath Industry Show, one of the largest trade shows in the country.

NKBA offers membership in four different categories: Industry, Associate, Student and Honorary. Industry memberships are broken into eleven different industry segments. For more information, visit NKBA at www.nkba.org.

THANK YOU TO OUR SPONSORS

The National Kitchen & Bath Association recognizes with gratitude the following companies who generously helped to fund the creation of this industry resource.

PATRONS

www.americanwoodmark.com

www.kohler.com

BENEFACTORS

www.ge.com

www.subzero.com

www.wolfappliance.com

CONTRIBUTOR

www.groheamerica.com

SUPPORTERS

www.nyloft.net

www.showhouse.moen.com

TOTO®

www.totousa.com

DONORS

Rev-A-Shelf | **Viking Range** | **Whirlpool**

This book is intended for professional use by residential kitchen and bath designers. The procedures and advice herein have been shown to be appropriate for the applications described; however, no warranty (expressed or implied) is intended or given. Moreover, the user of this book is cautioned to be familiar with and to adhere to all manufacturers' planning, installation and use/care instructions. In addition, the user is urged to become familiar with and adhere to all applicable local, state and federal building codes, licensing and legislation requirements governing the user's ability to perform all tasks associated with design and installation standards, and to collaborate with licensed practitioners who offer professional services in the technical areas of mechanical, electrical and load bearing design as required for regulatory approval, as well as health and safety regulations.

Information about this book and other association programs
and publications may be obtained from the
National Kitchen & Bath Association
687 Willow Grove Street, Hackettstown, New Jersey 07840
Phone (800) 843-6522
www.nkba.org

ISBN 1-887127-52-6

First Edition 2006

Illustrations by: Jerry Germer

Top cover photo courtesy Diane Foreman, CKD – Redmond, WA
Bottom cover photo courtesy Ellen Cheever, CMKBD, ASID – Wilmington, DE

Published on behalf of NKBA by Fry Communications, Irvine, CA

Peer Reviewers

Timothy Aden, CMKBD	Jim Krengel, CMKBD
Julia Beamish, Ph.D, CKE	Chris LaSpada, CPA
Leonard V. Casey	Elaine Lockard
Ellen Cheever, CMKBD, ASID	Phyllis Markussen, Ed.D, CKE, CBE
Hank Darlington	Chris J Murphy, CKD, CBD, CKBI
Dee David, CKD, CBD	David Newton, CMKBD
Peggy Deras, CKD, CID	Roberta Null, Ph.D
Kimball Derrick, CKD	Michael J Palkowitsch, CMKBD
Tim DiGuardi	Paul Pankow, CKBI
Kathleen Donohue, CMKBD	Jack Parks
Gretchen L. Edwards, CMKBD	Kathleen R. Parrott, Ph.D, CKE
JoAnn Emmel, Ph.D	Al Pattison,CMKBD
Jerry Germer	Les Petrie, CMKBD
Pietro A. Giorgi, Sr., CMKBD	Becky Sue Rajala, CKD
Tom Giorgi	Betty L. Ravnik, CKD, CBD
Jerome Hankins, CKD	Robert Schaefer
Spencer Hinkle, CKD	Klaudia Spivey, CMKBD
Max Isley, CMKBD	Kelly Stewart, CMKBD
Mark Karas, CMKBD	Tom Trzcinski, CMKBD
Martha Kerr, CMKBD	Stephanie Witt, CMKBD

Kitchens are no longer just for cooking. They have evolved into social centers where several people interact in the preparation and enjoyment of food. Similarly, today's baths transcend the utilitarian functions of personal hygiene to become sanctuaries where occupants can relax and restore their physical and emotional well-being. A variety of new appliances, fixtures and control systems have emerged to help these rooms play their new expanded roles. Making these devices work to help kitchens and baths fulfill their expanded roles challenges each member of the building team. As a designer, you must not only know the basics of kitchen and bath equipment, but also keep abreast of changes that seem to come at an ever-increasing pace.

You have more resources to help you meet this challenge than ever before. For example, it's possible to get a basic grounding in all aspects of kitchen and bath design and construction from the books in the *Professional Resource Library* published by the National Kitchen & Bath Association (NKBA) and then get information on new products and systems instantly over the Internet.

NKBA's *Professional Resource Library* not only provides the basis for certification as a kitchen and bath designer, but also is a way of promoting current industry standards and developments, and recommending kitchen and bath design and construction improvements.

This book covers the mechanical and electrical systems and equipment necessary for the function of kitchens and baths. Because these rooms are part of a larger system—the house—it is impossible to grasp the workings of these spaces without some understanding of the mechanical and electrical systems of the house. For that reason we will work from the general to the specific. In plumbing, for example, we'll trace the path of water from the main in the street (or the well) into the house, through the water heater, piping and into the dishwasher, then follow the wastewater out into the sewer.

Because we aim to include design in all of North America, we include international (metric) units in parentheses after English units.

This book contains four parts. The first, "The Big Picture," covers general background information every designer needs to know to function successfully and to turn a design concept into reality, whether the project is a remodel or new home.

We next move into the systems that create comfort inside the home. These systems provide heating and cooling and ensure a constant supply of healthy indoor air.

Plumbing systems are the topics of part three. We begin with getting hot and cold water to the fixtures, continue with the systems that carry away wastewater and end with the fixtures and their plumbing requirements.

In the fourth part, we'll cover what any designer should know about the role electricity plays in getting power from the meter to the appliance, then explore some of the new and exciting lighting possibilities for kitchens and baths.

This book contains a list of resources you may wish to contact for further information, a glossary of terms and an index to make it a handy reference source.

NKBA hopes this book will not only provide you with the necessary basics of kitchen and bath mechanical and electrical systems, but will also inspire you to pursue your career as a designer with a desire to create excellent environments for your clients.

PART ONE: THE BIG PICTURE

We begin this journey into kitchen and bath mechanical and electrical systems by setting the scene in which you will be working. The first chapter gives an overview of the various designers and installers who play a role in the process and where you as a specialist designer fit into the team. Next, we cover the legal issues you must deal with in order to translate your designs from concepts on paper into physical realities.

CHAPTER 1: The Building Team

As a kitchen and bath designer, you won't be working alone. To begin with, you'll obviously need clients. Beyond that you'll depend on a number of other professionals and installers to realize your design concepts. You should know your own strengths and weaknesses and what specialists to call upon for project tasks outside your own expertise. Working smoothly with this team of building specialists will require courtesy, respect and patience. This chapter will give you an overview of some of the major players on the building team and where they fit in.

The teams that design and build commercial or industrial projects have narrower, more clearly-defined roles than those involved with residences. Architects and engineers basically design and then check from time to time to ensure that work is being constructed as specified. A general contractor manages the construction with subcontractors installing various parts.

With residences many variations are possible. The overall design may not come from an architect or building designer at all, but from a magazine or other source, sometimes adapted by a designer for the specific project. The same firm who installs it might design the heating system. The same holds true for electrical work. A general contractor or homebuilder may coordinate the various sub-parts. Or it may be left to the owner. And the owner often installs some of the work.

How do you fit in? There's no general answer. Before you do anything else with a project you should pin down the organizational model, who does what and who answers to whom.

GENERALIST DESIGNERS

The design process starts with a program statement that lists the client's needs and goals. Your task is to translate that program into a concept that can ultimately be built. Building design is a huge field that contains both generalists and specialists. The overall design may be entrusted to an architect or building designer who coordinates the work of the other specialized design professionals. The list of specialists required to fill out the team varies according to the size and type of project and may include engineers, landscape architects, interior designers and—here's where you fit in—kitchen and bath designers.

Architects

The role of architects has changed dramatically from the days when they were the "master builder" who orchestrated the entire production of a building, from design through the driving of the last nail. Today architects mostly design, with limited oversight responsibilities during the construction phase. To be called an architect one must be licensed by the state, which requires a professional degree, a supervised internship and successfully passing a professional examination. Even though trained as generalists, architects today are increasingly specializing in a niche, such as hospitals, prisons, schools or residences. Architects who do residential design may include the detailed design of kitchens and baths in the scope of their services or leave it to a specialist designer once the general concept has been established. In this case the specialist designer may work through the architect or, more likely, answer directly to the client.

Engineers

Like architects, engineers are licensed by the state and obtain their qualifications via a professional degree and professional exam. Most engineers specialize in an area such as mechanical, electrical, structural and civil engineering. Multi-story housing may require the services of any or all of these specialties. The majority of single-family housing gets built without the services of any engineer, except maybe for a civil engineer to survey the site. In high-end housing, mechanical engineers may be entrusted with the design of the heating, ventilating and air conditioning (HVAC) systems. An electrical engineer might design the power and lighting, communications and other electrical systems.

To work effectively with an engineer you will need a final layout of your portions of the house, along with the particular equipment that will be installed. If a mechanical engineer is charged with designing the HVAC or plumbing system be prepared to provide the engineer with any plumbing, ducting and power requirements for the fixtures and equipment you specify. Get these requirements from the catalogs and pass them along as soon as possible in the design process. If an architect is in charge of the overall design, you will probably communicate this information through him/her.

Building Designers

Unlike architects, building designers do not need professional licenses to practice, though they are limited to buildings of a certain type and/or size. Most specialize in residential design.

If you are called in to consult on a project for which a building designer has prepared the plans, you may work either for the designer or the client.

Kitchen and Bath Designers

Professional kitchen and bath designers work directly with the client. They develop a survey of the client's needs, measure the space, create the design and present specifications that are implemented by the many trades people involved in the project. Design skill levels and experience are so diverse that there are different certification levels for kitchen and bath designers available through the National Kitchen & Bath Association (NKBA). These certifications help other building professionals and consumers determine the competence of the kitchen or bath designer.

All NKBA certifications, whether Associate Kitchen and Bath Designer® (AKBD), Certified Kitchen Designer® (CKD), Certified Bath Designer® (CBD) or Certified Master Kitchen and Bath Designer® (CMKBD), require specific cumulative kitchen and bath design education and experience, in addition to passing a rigorous academic certification examination and practical design examination covering all facets of the kitchen and bath industry from home construction to the elements and principles of design.

Interior Designers

The design team for a high-end residential project may include an interior designer who specializes in organizing the spaces and specifying furnishings and color schemes. Some interior designers are licensed by states in order to be certified and as such they must satisfy specific training and qualification requirements. If an interior designer is involved with the project you should clarify the various design responsibilities early on. Confusion may result if the team members don't know how they fit into the team.

INSTALLERS

General Contractors

All building projects need someone to coordinate the various actors involved in the construction. Whoever takes on this important charge must obtain the building permit, schedule the construction, recruit the subcontractors (subs), usually pay them and oversee the construction. The task can be as daunting as herding cats. Owners who act as their own general contractor often encounter rough shoals—work that doesn't happen when it is supposed to, unforeseen costs and numerous other frustrations. Hiring a general contractor helps avoid these kinds of headaches. General contractors must pass an examination by the state to obtain a license to conduct business. However, even with a pro managing the show the owner can still reserve portions of the work to do himself, such as installing drywall or painting.

Plumbers

If you think of plumbers as the experts on systems that move water in and out of kitchens and baths, it's obvious how crucial these installers are to the project team. Plumbers need to know their way around the myriad of pipes, fittings and fixtures, while keeping up to date with the latest code provisions. To practice, they must pass a state-administered exam and obtain a license. It's in your interest to get to know a few plumbers in your area so you can consult with them when you confront plumbing-related questions in your design work. And naturally, the plumber on your project will need to know the layout and plumbing requirements of the kitchen and bath fixtures.

Electricians

Electricians are also indispensable to kitchen and bath projects. Their work begins where yours leaves off. If your design shows the proposed locations of power outlets and lighting fixtures, the electrician must make sure all of these devices work as intended. Like plumbers, electricians must be licensed and follow the latest provisions of a reference code, most likely the *National Electrical Code*. Electricians usually determine the circuiting arrangements in residential work. For this, they'll need to know the voltage requirements of large appliances and which lighting fixtures are low-voltage, along with any other electrical requirements.

Home Technology Specialists

Home electrical systems used to consist of a high-voltage power system and low-voltage telephone system. The power system brought power to the house via a service panel with circuits for power and lighting. A wiring network distributed the electricity to the various points of use. Telephone wiring was mounted to a box on the outside wall connected to one or more phones inside by low-voltage wiring.

The "smart house" came on the scene in the 1980s with low-voltage systems to control appliances and lighting automatically. The technology was slow to catch on, but has progressed steadily. Many of today's new homes contain some provisions for home automation, ranging from data wiring in the walls to complete home automation systems with programmable options capable of controlling a multitude of electronic devices. Not surprisingly, these systems are complicated enough to require specialist designers and installers—either electrical engineers specialized in home automation or the vendors themselves. Because these systems affect the whole house, it is in your interest to be aware of them and know how and where they fit into your kitchen and bath design.

As a kitchen and bath designer you play an important part in realizing a residential project. To do this effectively you need to first know your craft, understand the project and be able to work smoothly with the other players on the team.

CHAPTER 2: Codes and Permits

Any project you design must comply with the applicable local and national laws. The legal issues that affect a construction project can be substantial and often confusing. Still, you don't have to be a lawyer to sort them out. Just be aware of which laws apply and know where to go for information. For starters, most localities require a building permit for construction exceeding a certain size or value. The design and construction must comply with whatever building codes are in force. In this chapter we'll look at how code and permitting issues, particularly those that affect mechanical and electrical systems, affect you as a kitchen and bath designer.

BUILDING CODES

Designers often grump about building codes because they see them as obstacles to creativity. That's unfortunate because the intent of codes is to ensure good design, at least as far as health and safety issues are concerned. Codes achieve this by establishing uniform minimum standards that are constantly updated to reflect advances in technology and changes in society.

U.S. Building Codes

Until recently there were three so-called "model codes" in force in the U.S. that set standards for buildings of all types. The *BOCA National Building Code*, published by the Building Officials and Code Administrators International (BOCA) applied primarily in the Northeast and Midwest. The *Uniform Building Code*, published by the International Conference of Building Officials (ICBO), set standards for Western states. The *Southern Building Code*, published by the Southern Building Code Conference International (SBCCI) applied to the majority of Southern states. A fourth code, *One and Two Family Dwelling Code*, often called the "CABO code" after its publisher, the Council of American Building Officials (CABO), addressed issues of particular concern to detached houses and as such has been acceptable to all three model codes for residential construction.

Local municipalities called these codes "model" because they were conceived as models for further refinement or alteration. While some large cities have their own codes, most municipalities simply adopt the applicable model code as-is or amend it to suit local needs. For example, locations with inordinately high dangers from hurricanes, fire, or earthquakes may amend the model code with requirements that address the particular hazard.

One of the reasons the designers and installers haven't liked codes is the confusion resulting from their multiplicity. Responding to pressure from the building industry for a single unified building code that applied to all parts of the U.S., the various code agencies established an umbrella organization, the International Code Council (ICC) in 1994 to create such a code. The product, the *International Building Code 2003* has by now been adopted by most regional code agencies as a replacement for the former model codes.

The three model code organizations, BOCA, ICBO, and SBCCI, addressed issues of home design and construction in the *International Residential Code (IRC)*. The IRC covers one- and two-family detached dwellings and apartment buildings up to three stories. The *IRC* is used as a reference for the NKBA Planning Guidelines.

You can find out which codes apply in your area from the building department of the municipality.

CODES AFFECTING MECHANICAL AND ELECTRICAL SYSTEMS

Model building codes cover all aspects of building construction. As such, they include standards for mechanical and electrical systems. For example, the *IRC* contains a stand-alone set of standards, with chapters on plumbing, electrical, mechanical, fuel gas and energy. This level of information will probably satisfy your needs as a residential kitchen and bath designer. Even so there are specific codes in force that address mechanical and electrical issues in greater detail. These are intended for specialists, such as engineers and installers. They also serve as the standards by which local building inspectors evaluate conformance. One of the first things you should do as you are getting established is find out which codes apply in the area you intend to serve.

Plumbing Codes

Because piping systems are so indispensable to kitchens and baths, designers need to know the basics of hot and cold water supply, drainage and venting, as well as the applicable code standards. The *Uniform Plumbing Code (UPC)*, which spells out these standards in great detail, is the bible of plumbers in the U.S. and the source most used by municipalities. The UPC is adopted by jurisdictions primarily in the western U.S.

9

Electrical Codes

The National Electrical Code (NEC) has been adopted by most states, cities and municipalities as the most widely used and accepted reference for all electrical installations. The NEC is continually updated to provide the most recent data designers and installers need for electrical work. Much of the data is aimed at engineers and electricians, but portions address kitchen and bath equipment safety, such as ground fault circuit interrupter (GFCI) devices, a must for receptacles in wet areas.

Energy Codes

Since kitchen and bath appliances and equipment need an energy source to make them run, the cost and availability of energy is a natural concern of designers and specifiers. It has taken on more importance since the energy crises of the 1970s. Fortunately, the ensuing shortages sparked new ways to conserve energy and spawned new technologies for utilizing renewable energy from solar, wind and geothermal sources in homes. To encourage conservation in buildings, government agencies developed standards that found their way into various model energy codes. The **Model Energy Code (MEC)** was developed by the Council of American Building Officials (CABO) in cooperation with the National Conference of States on Building Codes & Standards and first published in 1986. In 1992, the MEC became the reference code for the National Energy Policy Act. In 1995, CABO transferred ownership and all rights to the MEC to a successor organization, the International Code Council (ICC). In 1998 the ICC published an updated edition incorporating all approved changes to the '95 MEC.

The new edition is called the *International Energy Conservation Code (IECC)*. There are two ways to ensure compliance with the code. The easiest, but not necessarily most economical, is to simply follow a set of **prescriptive standards**, which state levels of insulation, glazing requirements and other minimum requirements. The more complicated way to comply is submit calculations that ensure the building as a whole meets the **performance standards** of the code. The performance-standard route allows designers more flexibility if they are willing to and capable of submitting the engineering calculations. In any case, this responsibility falls to the building designer or engineer, not the kitchen or bath designer.

There are, however, sections of the code of which you should be aware. These sections require materials and equipment to be identified so that code compliance can be determined. Manufacturer manuals for all installed heating and cooling equipment and water heating equipment must be provided.

Many states and municipalities have since either developed their own energy conservation requirements or have adopted a model code. Forty states currently have energy codes in force.

Fire Safety Codes

The most widely accepted fire safety code in use in the U.S. is the *Life Safety Code*, published by the National Fire Protection Association. Chapter 24 of the *Life Safety Code* addresses means of egress for one- and two-story homes. Provisions for mechanical and electrical equipment are included in Chapter 9.

CANADIAN BUILDING CODES

As in the U.S., Canadian model national building, fire and plumbing codes are prepared under a central agency then adopted and enforced by the provincial and territorial authorities who have jurisdiction. The following table indicates which codes are in force in the various provinces and territories.

Province or Territory	National Building Code	National Fire Code	National Plumbing Code	Provincial Codes based on model national codes
Northwest Territories, Nunavut and Yukon	P	P	P	
British Columbia				P
Alberta				P
Saskatchewan	P	P	P	
Manitoba	P	P	P	
Ontario				P
Quebec		M		P
Newfoundland and Labrador		P		
New Brunswick	M	P	P	
Nova Scotia	P	M	P	
Prince Edward Island	M		P	P

Legend:
P   Province-wide adoption of code, as-is, or modified
M   Adoption of code by municipalities

Canadian energy standards are published in the *Model National Energy Code of Canada for Houses (MNECH)*, which allows designers to choose the degree of energy efficiency that is appropriate for specific climates and fuel types. The MNECH applies to residential buildings of three stories or fewer and additions of more than 10 m². Because of the cold climates of Canadian provinces, the emphasis is on high insulation and air-tightness.

PERMITS AND INSPECTIONS

Local municipalities issue building permits as a way to tax new construction or remodeling and track compliance with any prevailing codes in force. Localities differ as to what type and size of project requires a permit, as well as what's required to obtain one. Drawings showing the proposed construction are usually required, so be prepared to have your portion of the work in submittal form. A straightforward interior remodeling project may require no other documentation. It's usually up to the owner or general contractor to obtain the permit. The application fee is normally a percentage of the construction value of the project.

Plumbing and electrical work often requires separate permits. For each such permit, there will be inspections at various milestones in the installation. It is the responsibility of the general contractor to notify the building department at the completion of each phase of work requiring an inspection. The first inspection usually occurs when the rough framing is complete. A second one for plumbing and electrical work happens when the rough-in (wiring and piping) is complete but before any wall finishes have been installed. Finishes, in this case, means surfaces that enclose the systems, such as wallboard or subfloor material. If your responsibilities extend beyond design to include oversight during the construction phase, you will need to be aware of the required inspection milestones and make sure they occur at a time that will prevent construction delays. There may be a final inspection when all construction is complete, as a condition of granting an occupancy permit or certificate of occupancy (CO).

WORKING WITH BUILDING OFFICIALS

Working with local building departments can be a nightmare or a walk in the park. In general, the bigger the municipality, the larger the bureaucracy you'll face in the permitting and inspection processes. Know who you will be dealing with at the outset to avoid hassles. The inspector in a small, rural area may be a part-timer with another job or occupation. Such an inspector will probably have only minimal involvement with the project. But a larger city will have a separate building department staffed with experts in code issues. Here are some tips to help you smooth the path:

- Find out which codes are in force and get a copy of them. Familiarize yourself with the provisions of the codes that affect your sphere of operation.

- Visit the local building department to familiarize yourself about the process and obtain information about permits, fees and inspection procedures.

- Get a copy of the local zoning ordinance and check its provisions for each project you propose.

- While the project is still in the planning/design stage, take preliminary drawings in to get input and advice. You won't get written approval at that stage, but the officials appreciate being consulted while there is still time for changes and you can use their input to make sure your design doesn't fly in the face of local laws or regulations.

- Make sure plans you submit have any professional stamp required (architect, engineer, surveyor).

- Notify the appropriate inspectors in a timely manner when inspections are due.

- Don't be confrontational with building officials. Listen to their concerns, express your own and seek compromise. Sometimes it pays to let some time lapse and tempers cool before you respond. If you feel you are in over your head, seek outside advice of architects, engineers or attorneys before taking on the building department.

Familiarity with the legal requirements of construction will help you see them less as obstacles to the design or construction of a project and more as simply another ingredient in the process that you can deal with successfully.

PART TWO: HVAC SYSTEMS

Except for the southern tip of Florida, most homes in North America need some means of heating. It may be as simple as a wood stove or as complicated as a multi-zone central heating system. With good design, many homes can get much of their heat from the sun. In this chapter we'll scan the variety of ways North Americans heat their homes and how the choices affect the areas of your design.

CHAPTER 3: Heating Systems

COMFORT AND HEAT

You can understand heating systems better if you start with some understanding of what we mean by *heat* and how it relates to *comfort*. To begin, the sensation of comfort varies from person to person, with age, activity level and the conditions of the atmosphere surrounding them. These conditions have been quantified and refined over many years of study by scientists and are displayed in a psychometric chart known as the **Human Comfort Zone**, shown on Figure 3.1. The chart is based on the comfort felt by people exposed to various temperatures, humidity levels and air movement. To make a room comfortable, the heating and cooling equipment must respond to the variables in the chart and do so dependably, quietly and efficiently—a tall order.

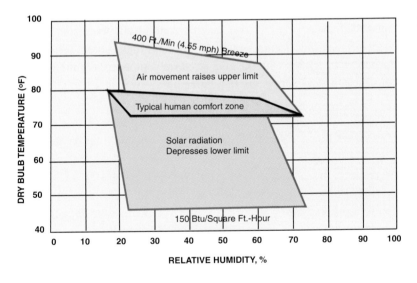

Figure 3.1 The atmospheric conditions that define human comfort can be graphed. Most people feel comfortable in the purple-colored zone. With ventilation, comfort is possible at higher air temperatures (upper zone of graph). Similarly, solar heat extends the comfort zone downward to around 46°F.

Temperature, one of the variables in the chart, measures the amount of heat in the air. Heat is a form of energy that travels from a warmer to a colder place. It travels in three ways: conduction, convection and radiation. When you touch the handle of your car door on a January morning it feels cold because heat is passing directly from your hand to the handle by **conduction**. Now imagine holding a lit match just above the palm of your hand. The warmth you feel comes from the match transporting its heat by **radiation**. If you hold your hand above the flame at some distance, you can still feel its warmth, though in this case the heat more likely comes from the air heated by the flame and warms your hand by **convection**.

Home heating systems employ all three modes of heat transfer, alone or in combination and because they often rely on more than one mode, it is handier to classify them by the medium they use to distribute the heat. This concept will become clearer as we look at the various ways to heat a house.

CONSERVATION FIRST

All heating systems need some form of energy to create warmth. Regardless of the energy source, the amount of energy needed varies greatly with the climate, the solar exposure of the house and how the house is designed and built. With the cost of energy growing and the uncertainty of supply of fossil fuels in the future, homeowners will benefit from anything designers can do to promote energy conservation. Most of the decisions that affect the construction of the home will probably be made by the time you enter the picture as a kitchen or bath designer, but you can still promote conservation by the equipment and appliances you specify. And a basic understanding of energy-conserving design strategies will help make sure your part of the design integrates with the energy conservation goals of the home's construction. An energy-efficient home has:

- An energy-conserving envelope.

- Ways to use natural energies to heat, cool and light the interior.

- Energy-efficient equipment.

Heat passes in and out of the envelope (walls and roof) by conduction, radiation and convection. Good insulation, efficient windows and sealing cracks and openings all help create an energy-conserving envelope. The next step is to draw upon the natural energies that are usually available and either free or inexpensive for the taking. For example, breezes can provide much or all of the cooling in most climates. Good window design and location not only capture favorable breezes but also provide an escape route during the cool night for hot air trapped inside. The sun can provide much of a home's heating, as well as natural lighting. For more detail on these strategies, see the discussion in Chapter 4 of NKBA's *Residential Construction* book. Finally, select energy-efficient equipment to save your clients money on whatever fuel they use for heat. You'll find more on energy-efficient appliances in NKBA's *Kitchen and Bath Products* book.

HOME HEATING WITH THE SUN

Using solar energy to provide all or part of a home's space heat started with the Greeks and Romans but didn't see much activity in industrial countries until the 1970s, when oil from the Middle East suddenly got expensive and spurred interest in conservation and renewable energies. There are two techniques for using the sun to heat houses: **active** and **passive**. Active systems use rooftop collectors to trap solar heat into a liquid medium or air that circulates the heated liquid into the house, via heat exchangers and fans. Because of the unfavorable appearance of solar collectors on the roof as well as the cost, complexity and high maintenance requirements of active systems, their appeal has mainly been limited to southern locations where they can provide most of the heat needed for the house in winter and heat water for swimming pools in the warm season. In other areas, the passive approach has proven more popular.

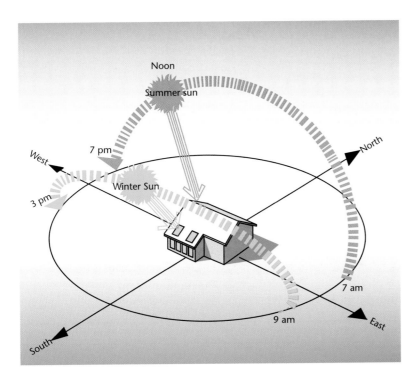

Figure 3.2 The path of the sun in summer is higher than at winter. To get the most benefit from the sun's light and warmth, a house should be sited so that its long façade faces southward. Include sufficient glazing along this façade to capture the sun's rays.

A house that uses passive solar heat starts with an energy-conserving shell, as mentioned above. The ideal passive solar house has a compact footprint, with the longest side facing as close to due south as possible. Most passive solar houses in North America collect the sun's heat directly or indirectly, through a sunspace.

Direct Gain

By far the simplest way to get heat from the sun into a house is through the windows. But the windows have to face the sun, which means southward for houses in the Northern Hemisphere. Solar rays penetrate the glass and strike an opaque surface, which radiates the energy as heat to the space. If the surface is a dark-colored, dense material, such as brick, stone, tile or colored concrete, some of the heat is trapped- or stored-in the material and slowly released, an ideal situation for the times when the sun isn't shining. Windows for passive solar heating should be energy-efficient, preferably with low-E coating. Roof overhangs or other shading devices should be part of the design to protect against overheating in the warmer months.

Figure 3.3 Direct gain is the simplest way to trap solar heat. A house designed for this approach has ample south glazing to collect solar light and heat and a means of shading to block unwanted solar heat in the warm seasons. In this illustration, the roof overhangs just enough to block the summer rays, while admitting the lower-angle winter rays. A massive floor, such as a concrete slab, can absorb solar heat to even out day-to-night temperatures.

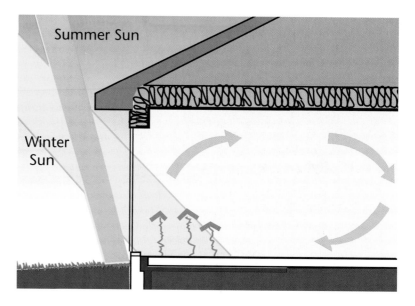

Sunspace

The sun's heat can also be collected indirectly, through an adjoining room, or "sunspace." This approach has the advantage of greater control of heat flow. Because the space can be isolated from main living area at night, it won't draw heat from the house on cold, winter nights (though it may be desirable to either allow some heat from the house to enter the sunspace or provide an auxiliary heater on the coldest nights to keep plants from freezing). Sunspaces can serve functional needs, as well as provide solar heat. Properly designed, they can make a welcoming entry/mud room and/or a place to grow plants. As with direct-gain systems, sunspace design must provide means for shading during warm seasons.

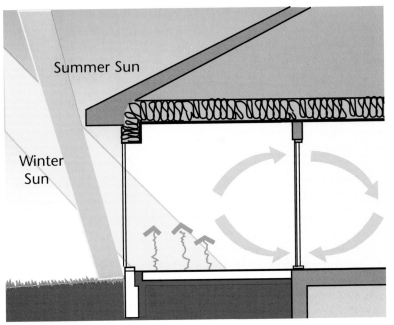

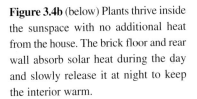

Figure 3.4 (left) A sunspace traps solar heat in the same way as direct gain (Figure 3.3), but supplies it to the house indirectly, through doors or windows that can control the amount of heat transfer into or out of the house.

Figure 3.4b (below) Plants thrive inside the sunspace with no additional heat from the house. The brick floor and rear wall absorb solar heat during the day and slowly release it at night to keep the interior warm.

Figure 3.4a This sunspace serves as a bright, cheerful rear entrance to a two-story Colonial house. The tall vertical glazing faces south, to capture the low winter sunlight.

HEATING FUELS

Most homes draw upon an energy source other than the sun for their heat and even solar-heated homes typically rely on another source for backup heat. Sadly, we are dependent on fossil fuels for home heat. Natural and bottled gas provides the bulk of home heating in North America, with electricity the next most common source. Wood and other renewable energy sources make up the rest of the energy pie.

Gas

Think of gas as molecules in motion. Gas molecules fill any containing vessel, with equal pressure in all directions. Just as water flows from a higher to lower level and heat flows from a hotter to cooler body, gas flows from a place of higher pressure to one of lower pressure.

Gas made its debut in homes in the 1900s as a fuel for lighting. It subsequently became a common energy source for cooking, space heating and water heating. These uses continue today, with some newer applications gaining ground, such as gas-powered refrigerators, heaters, fireplaces and outdoor barbeques. Because gas reserves are apparently ample, this energy source will surely play a big part in residential applications in future years. Its appeal is heightened by the fact that gas is a convenient fuel to use. When you turn on the stove burner, you get immediate heat. It's also relatively clean burning, producing mainly carbon dioxide in the process.

In North America we measure heat content in British Thermal Units (Btu's). Countries using the metric system use calories. One Btu is the amount of heat energy required to raise the temperature of one pound of water by one degree Fahrenheit. This is roughly equivalent to the heat you get by burning a wooden match. A standard **cubic foot of gas**, as defined by the American Gas Association, is the quantity of gas contained in one cubic foot of volume at a barometric pressure of 30-inches of mercury at a temperature of 60° F. Thus, the heating value of any particular gas is the number of Btu's it produces per cubic foot.

Gas comes into our homes either through public utility pipelines (natural gas) or is delivered in trucks to storage tanks in the yard (liquefied petroleum or LP gas). **Natural gas** is mostly methane tapped from wells sunk into gas-bearing sands and piped to a local utility company, which distributes it to homes through its own municipal pipe network. A meter at the point of entry measures the quantity of gas consumed by a home in any given time period.

LP gas may be either butane or propane or a mixture of the two. It may come from natural gas sources or from the distillation process of an oil refinery. In either case, LP gas is liquefied under pressure and shipped in tank trucks. Local gas companies distribute the product to consumers, filling their on-site tanks by means of hoses attached to the tank truck. Consumers are either billed for each fill or according to a monthly arrangement.

Because natural or LP gas is constantly under pressure, any leaks in the containers—the storage tank and distribution piping—pose a fire danger. Two requirements help minimize this danger:

- All gas piping must be black steel or copper, with joints connected by compression, rather than soldered, fittings.

- A disagreeable odor added to the gas alerts occupants of any leak.

You can detect the distinctive odor in the instant between turning on the knob of a gas range and when it ignites.

Electricity

All matter is made up of atoms. The nucleus, the center of the atom, contains positively charged particles called protons and uncharged particles called neutrons. Negatively charged particles called electrons surround the atom. When an outside force upsets the balance between protons and electrons, an atom may gain or lose an electron. When electrons are "lost" from an atom, the free movement of these electrons constitutes an electric current. We get electricity from the conversion of other sources of energy, like coal, natural gas, oil, nuclear power and other natural sources. Before electricity generation began over 100 years ago, kerosene lamps lit houses, iceboxes kept food cooled and wood- or coal-burning stoves heated the rooms. Electrical power today is universally used to power equipment, lighting and heating. Slightly less than a third of all homes get their heat from electricity.

Electricity is measured in units of power called **watts**. Because a single watt is a very small amount when it comes to most uses, we use units of a thousand watts, or **kilowatts**. The usage over time needs another variable, the hours of usage. Thus, the units of electrical power are measured in **kilowatt-hours**, or **kWh**. One kWh is equal to the energy of 1,000 watts working for one hour. Most electricity in North America is produced from turbines, powered by moving water, nuclear

21

energy or a fuel such as coal, natural gas or oil. A very small but increasing amount is converted directly from the sun by photovoltaic cells mounted to face into the sun. Wind and biomass (the burning of garbage) can also generate electricity, but account for a very small percentage of the total.

Electricity from the generating plant travels along cables to a transformer on a nearby power pole. The transformer steps the voltage down from that carried on the line and delivers 220 or 240 volts to the service panel in the house.

Oil

Heating oil is one of the end products of the refining of crude oil. It is heavier than the lightest products of the refining process— gasoline, for example—but lighter than motor oils and tar. No. 2 heating oil is the third most dominant energy source for home heating in the U.S. and fuel of choice for 40 percent of the homes in the Northeast/Mid-Atlantic region of the U.S., as well as much of Canada. As with LP gas, heating oil is delivered to homes by tank trucks.

Heating oil burns clean, with minimal exhaust emissions, if burned in efficient equipment. Compared to other fuels in the region, heating oil is usually the most economical alternative.

Despite short-term fluctuations, oil heat prices have remained largely stable over the past 20 years. Measured in constant dollars, heating oil prices have actually declined in the fourteen largest residential oil-consuming states, while natural gas prices in these states have increased significantly. Today, oil and gas prices in the region are roughly at parity and both are well below the costs of electricity.

Heating oil has two safety pluses as well. First, unlike gas, when oil leaks occur, they are non-explosive. Second, heating oil will not burn in a liquid state. It must first be vaporized to fire inside a burner. Finally, a large quantity of oil can be stored safely on site.

Wood

The warmth and good feeling that comes from sitting near a fireplace or wood-burning stove has ensured a place for wood as a heating fuel since early times. While only a small portion of today's homes (4% in the U.S.) rely on wood heat for their primary fuel, many homeowners want a wood-burning fireplace or stove as a secondary heat source. Hardwood is the preferred type of wood for fuel, because it yields more heat per unit of wood than softwood.

Firewood is measured in **cords**. One cord is the quantity of wood that can be stacked in a volume measuring 4 feet x 4 feet x 8 feet. It is trucked to most home sites in random lengths, to be cut and split by the homeowner, or as pre-cut and split lengths of around two feet long, ready for burning. Wood fuel is also available in the form of pellets compressed from sawdust.

Wood as a heating fuel requires much more involvement on the part of the homeowner than other fuels. Even when delivered cut and split, wood must be stored and loaded into the appliance. The ashes must be removed. Unfortunately, burning wood also emits hundreds of chemical compounds and particulates that pollute the air, many of which pose serious risks to people with respiratory ailments. For that reason, government agencies have taken a variety of measures to minimize the hazard. Some municipalities restrict wood heating in times of unacceptable air quality. Others restrict or ban wood-burning appliances in new construction. Some states have air pollutant emission standards and certification programs for wood-burning appliances, modeled on those of the EPA. The standards have encouraged manufacturers to equip their appliances with catalytic converters or to develop designs that meet the emission requirements. One positive outcome of the improved products is that they also use less wood to produce the same amount of heat.

Coal

Not so long ago meals in almost every home were cooked on a cast iron stove that burned coal while a coal-burning furnace in the basement heated the home. Both of these vanished when gas, oil and electricity—all more convenient and cleaner burning fuels—became widely available. Today coal is seeing a minor comeback in some space-heating stoves but is rarely used beyond that in residences.

The term "coal" describes a variety of fossilized plant materials with varying heating values, ash-melting temperatures, sulfur content and many other chemical and physical properties. **Anthracite**, the most common type of coal for home heating, has a heat value of nearly 15,000 Btus-per-pound. **Bituminous coal** is a softer, dirtier-burning coal used primarily to generate electricity and make coke for the steel industry.

None of the fuels mentioned so far can heat a house without some means of converting the energy of the fuel into useful heat and getting the heat to where it's needed in the house. The devices for accomplishing these tasks make up a *heating system*. In the following sections we'll scan the various types of heating systems in today's homes.

FORCED-AIR HEATING SYSTEMS

Forced-air systems heat the house through convection. There are two parts to the system, a central heating device—the furnace—and a distribution network—the ducts and accessories. Forced-air heating has both pros and cons.

On the upside, the ductwork in forced-air heating systems can do double duty to distribute cold air during the hot season via a central air-conditioner attached to the system. However, constantly moving air can worsen the condition of people with respiratory disorders.

The Furnace

The heart of a forced-air heating system is the furnace. Cold air from the rooms is moved, via return-air ducts usually located in a central position, such as a hallway. The cold air travels to the furnace through a **return air plenum**, passing through a filter that removes dust and other particles, and then into a **heat exchanger**. Most furnaces are gas-fired, but other fuels include oil, coal, wood and electricity. The choice depends on the cost and availability of each fuel source in a particular region.

In a gas furnace, natural or LP gas is piped to a burner inside the combustion chamber, where it mixes with air. A pilot light, spark or a similar device controlled by a thermostat ignites a flame that heats up a metal box called the heat exchanger, through which room air flows. The flame requires a source of oxygen, or combustion air, which can come from the ambient air, if the furnace is open to it and the walls are not too tightly sealed. The trend, however, is toward more tightly sealed homes designed to conserve heat. These tight houses should be provided with a source of combustion air. This air is ducted from the outside directly into the burner and never mixes with the ambient air of the house. Gasses given off by the burners exhaust to the outdoors via a flue through the roof or—with newer, high-efficiency models—through a wall. A separate coil may run through the combustion chamber to heat water for use in the home.

Electric forced-air furnaces use resistance heating elements rather than burners to heat the air in the heat exchanger. Because they heat air by moving it over a resistance coil rather than a flame, these systems need neither a source of combustion air nor venting for flue gasses. Even with these pluses, the high cost of electricity in many regions makes electric furnaces the least economical option.

Forced-air furnaces come in two versions, according to their position in relation to the ductwork. An **upflow furnace** draws cool air into the bottom and blows warmed air out the top into heating ductwork. This type of furnace is usually installed in a basement, utility area or an out-of-the-way closet. If installed in the basement, an upflow furnace delivers heat to two or more floors above. Another location is the main floor of a single floor house whose ducts run through the attic.

If it is necessary to deliver heat to floors below the furnace, a **downflow** or **counterflow furnace** is the proper choice. A downflow furnace takes cool air in at the top and blows warm air toward the bottom.

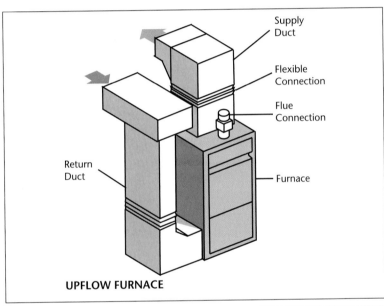

UPFLOW FURNACE

Figure 3.5 The choice of upflow or downflow furnace depends on its location. An upflow furnace is typically in the basement and supplies heated air overhead to the floors above. A downflow furnace is located above the floors it serves.

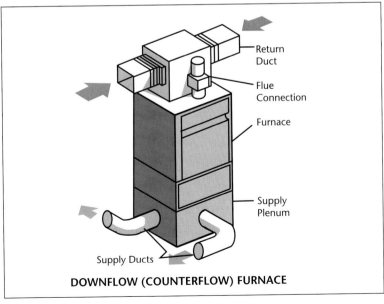

DOWNFLOW (COUNTERFLOW) FURNACE

Today's furnaces are much more efficient than their predecessors. The standard measure of their efficiency is the **Annual Fuel Utilization Efficiency (AFUE)**, expressed as a percentage. The AFUE compares the amount of fuel converted to space heat to the amount of fuel consumed. To qualify for the "Energy Star" label of the EPA, a furnace must:

- Meet or exceed 90% AFUE energy-efficiency ratings.

- Have a Manufacturer's Limited Warranty.

- Be manufactured by an Energy Star partner.

Duct Systems

The fan in a forced-air furnace blows heated air from the heat exchanger into a **supply plenum**. Smaller sized **branch ducts** tap into the plenum to supply warm air to the rooms through diffusers (also called registers). Ducts may be round or rectangular—or both—and made of metal or fiberboard. Typically located below the floor they serve, they may also be run above the ceiling, though delivering the warm air downward is less efficient than blowing it upward, since warm air naturally tends to rise. Ducts located in a cold attic or crawlspace must be insulated to prevent heat loss. In below-floor systems, diffusers mount either on the floor or on a wall near the floor. Diffusers in ceiling-ducted systems may be mounted either in the ceilings or near the floor, if a duct can be run down from the duct through a wall space.

Figure 3.6 A forced-air heating system supplies warm air through diffusers along the periphery of the house. Cool air returns to the furnace through a return vent typically located in a hallway

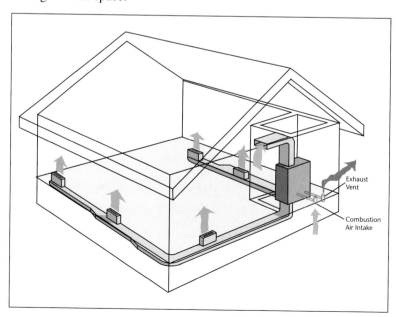

Exhaust Vent

Combustion Air Intake

Locating diffusers in kitchens and baths is often more difficult than other rooms for several reasons. First, these rooms—especially baths—are smaller and equipment or fixtures take up a good deal of the wall space. On the upside, these rooms don't usually need as much supplemental heat as other rooms. The occupants are usually moving around in a kitchen or bath, rather than sitting or lying in bed. And cooking, washing and bathing generate heat themselves, often too much. Still, kitchens and baths should be provided with at least one diffuser. For rooms with no convenient locations on a floor or wall, there are special diffusers that mount in the kickspace below a cabinet.

Air supplied to the rooms must somehow find its way back to the source. Room doors should be sized to leave a gap of an inch or so at the bottom to allow the air to circulate. A grille located in a central position, such as a hallway, picks up the return air and carries it back to the furnace via a return duct that feeds into a return air plenum.

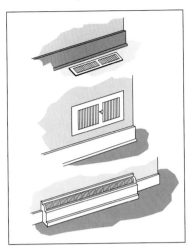

Figure 3.7 (below) Diffusers (registers) for air heating and cooling systems come in many shapes and sizes and can be located in any interior surface.

HYDRONIC HEATING SYSTEMS

The word *hydronic* comes from the Greek *hydro*, meaning water and hydronic systems are sometimes called *hot water* systems. Where forced-air heating systems heat room air directly, hydronic systems heat water that heats the home indirectly via a network of piping running around the periphery of the house (**baseboard systems**) or tubing arrayed below the floor (**radiant floor systems**).

Baseboard Systems

Hot water baseboard systems have replaced steam heating systems in new construction and can retrofit steam heating systems in older houses, making use of the existing radiators and piping. A **boiler** heats water in a combustion chamber. The water circulates through a network of piping to the rooms and transfers its heat via **fintube diffusers**, an assembly of aluminum plates attached to the pipe. The plates greatly expand the area of heated metal exposed to the air, thereby increasing the heat transfer to the room air. Though some heat is radiated, most of the heat comes from convection, as room air passes up and over the plates. Hydronic baseboard systems have both pros and cons, when compared to forced-air heating.

Pros:

• The initial cost of hydronic is less than forced air, because the distribution piping and diffusers cost much less than duct work.

• Lacking ductwork, hydronic systems save much more space and are easier to fit through the structure—a boon to remodeling and additions.

• Because hydronic systems don't move air around, they benefit persons with respiratory ailments.

Cons:

• A separate ductwork system must be installed if air conditioning is desired.

• Hydronic systems contain no filters to cleanse the air.

Hydronic systems appeal mostly to homeowners in heating—rather than cooling—dominated climates, where the ductwork can do double duty as a conduit for cooled air in the summer.

Gas and oil are both used as fuel for **standard boilers** in hydronic systems. Oil is more common, due to the reasons cited previously. If gas is the source, it comes either from an underground pipe connected to a natural gas utility or from an LP tank in the yard. Oil is stored in a tank inside the house near the boiler and gravity-fed into the boiler through a small-diameter pipe. When the thermostat triggers a call for heat, a nozzle in the burner mixes the oil with air and sprays the mixture into the combustion chamber, where a pilot ignites it. The flame wraps around the cast iron sections containing water, heating it to the target level. A circulator pump (or pumps in multi-zone systems) then pumps the hot water through the distribution network. As in forced-air furnaces, boilers may also contain a secondary loop of piping to heat water for domestic use. Boilers of this type are called combination boilers.

Standard boilers achieve efficiencies of upwards of 85%. A newer type called a **condensing boiler** reaches efficiencies of up to 95%, by improving the way the fuel is burned. A second heat exchanger recoups some of the heat from the hot exhaust gasses to preheat the water in the boiler system. When working at peak efficiency, the water vapor produced in the combustion process condenses back into liquid form. This condensate is piped away through non-corrosive piping because it is acidic. Condensing boilers run on either gas or oil. They have one added benefit over standard boilers: they don't need an exhaust flue or chimney. The relatively low temperatures of the combustion gas produce low temperature carbon dioxide that can be vented directly to the outside through a 2-inch diameter PVC pipe. A second pipe or concentric pipe around the exhaust pipe brings combustion air into the fire chamber, making the operation of the unit independent of the air supply in the home, a boon to tightly-sealed energy-efficient houses. While condensing boilers cost more initially than standard boilers, the difference is eventually recouped in fuel savings. And doing away with a chimney saves on costs while making for more flexibility in interior planning.

Figure 3.8 An oil-fired boiler and its components.

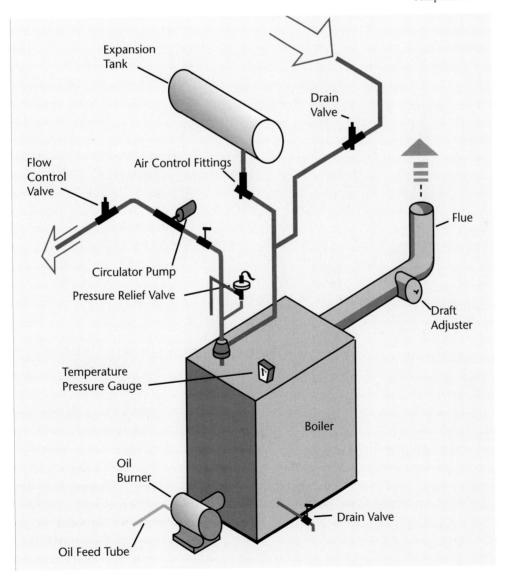

Heated water circulates through copper piping that runs around the perimeter of the house. The simplest circuit is a simple loop with a continuous pipe that connects each fintube diffuser mounted near the baseboard in each room. The obvious disadvantage of this **series perimeter loop** layout is that the water temperature drops at each fintube and gets progressively cooler toward the end of the run. An improved version is the **one-pipe** system, which allows the main supply/return pipe to bypass each fintube. A special fitting or valve at each fintube can control the flow. A **two-pipe** loop is better still. With a separate supply and return loop, water nearly at boiler temperature is supplied to each fintube without being cooled by passing through the previous one or accepting cooler return water.

Figure 3.9a Three arrangements for hydronic circuits. The one-pipe series perimeter loop (A), while the simplest, is not the best, since water is cooler by the time it reaches diffusers at the end of the loop.

Figure 3.9b The one-pipe system (B) overcomes this drawback by giving the supply pipe a straight run. Valves can be added at the end of each diffuser to control its heat.

Figure 3.9c The two-pipe reverse return system (C) is better still, since boiler temperature water is supplied to each diffuser and cooler water returns via a separate line.

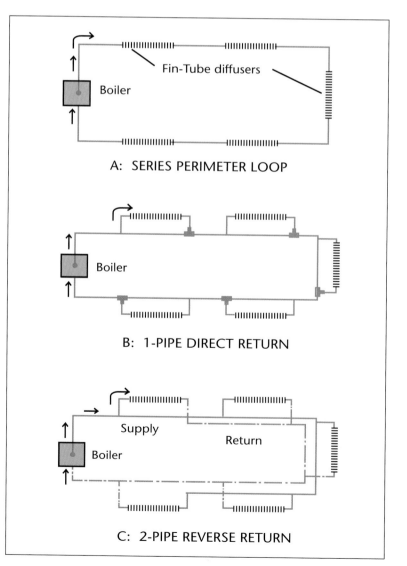

The fintube diffusers that run around the walls of a room in hydronic systems are easily located in rooms with a lot of unobstructed wall space, such as living rooms and bedrooms. But the base cabinetry in kitchens eats up most of the available wall space, leaving little for fintube diffusers. Fortunately, there are special heating units that fit in the toe space under base cabinets. The hydronic version uses electricity to heat water that runs through tubing. An all-electric version uses a resistance coil. In both types, a fan forces air out through a grille in the toe space into the room.

Radiant Floor Systems

Why not heat people directly instead of heating the air around them, as forced air and hydronic baseboard systems do? This is exactly what radiant heating does. Radiant floor systems also need a piping network to deliver heat, but the piping is expanded over the surface of the floor, making the whole floor the heat diffuser. With a much larger distribution area, the heat can be delivered at a lower temperature. The floor radiates heat directly to the occupants, rather than heating room air first. People feel warmer, even with the lower air temperature. Ads for radiant floor heating drive this point home by showing happy homeowners lounging about on radiant-heated floors in their bare feet. The approach has other pluses, as well. Lower thermostat settings relate to energy savings. The tubing can be coupled with active solar collectors to take advantage of solar energy. Radiant floor heating is quiet, needs no registers in the walls or floor and doesn't blow dust around, as does forced air. On the downside, it costs more than other systems and some experts argue that the additional cost would be better spent with a more energy-efficient envelope. Also, radiant floors work best with hard, preferably masonry, floor surfaces. This feature makes radiant floors especially attractive heating options for baths and to a lesser degree, kitchens, for the following reasons:

- Cabinetry and fixtures in kitchens and baths limit the locations for heat diffusers.

- Kitchens and baths are more likely to have tiled, or at least uncarpeted, floors.

- The occupants are barefoot, much of the time, in baths.

As with other hydronic systems radiant floor heating begins with a gas- or oil-fired boiler to heat the water. The warm water typically circulates through loops of closely spaced plastic tubing, typically cross-linked polybutylene (PBX). The loops are organized into zones,

31

with the supply to each zone regulated by a distribution manifold near the boiler. The plastic distribution tubing can be imbedded in concrete slabs, if insulated below. In wood floors, the tubing can snug up to the underside of the subfloor, between the joists, or be imbedded into a 2-inch layer of lightweight concrete (or gypsum concrete) topping poured over the subfloor. Of course the topping costs and adds weight, which, in turn drives up the cost of the supporting structure.

Figure 3.10 A simple radiant floor heating system delivers hot water to the floor through one loop, returning cooled water to the boiler through another.

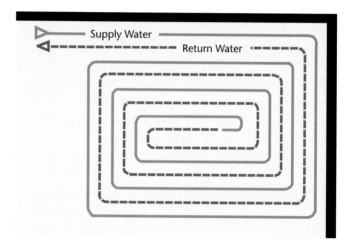

Figure 3.11 Tubing for radiant floor systems can be imbedded in a concrete slab or attached to the underside of a wood floor. Metal plates around the tubing help transfer heat from the tube to the wood.

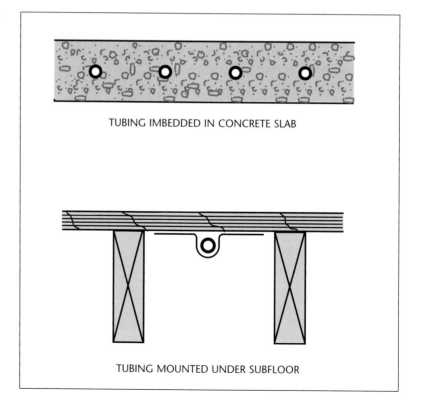

ELECTRIC HEATING SYSTEMS

Electricity passed through poor conductors generates heat by its resistance, an elegant and simple component of a heating system. Unfortunately, it's also one of the most expensive today, which explains why electric heating takes a backseat to other fuels. (Another form of heating with electricity is discussed in the next chapter in connection with heat pumps). Nonetheless, electric resistance heating may be practical in some situations, such as a bathroom addition with no way to tie into the home's main heating system.

Electric radiant heating can be installed in floors, as in hydronic systems, as well as walls and ceilings, which makes it an option to consider for baths that are hard to heat with other alternatives. Electric radiant heating systems use resistance cable imbedded behind room finish materials to convert electrical energy to radiant heat. The system is simple, quiet and clean and heats occupants directly, rather than the room air, as with hydronic radiant systems.

Electric forced-air furnaces provide heat by moving air across resistance heating elements. The hot air is then fan-forced through ducts in the same way as was described for forced-air systems. The main advantages are the absence of vents or flues and no need to worry about keeping the LP gas tank or oil tank filled.

Baseboard convectors are likely the simplest way to heat with electricity. Electricity runs through resistance cable inside metal tubing. Fins encase the tubing as in fintube hydronic diffusers to conduct the heat out of the cable, which heats the room by convection.

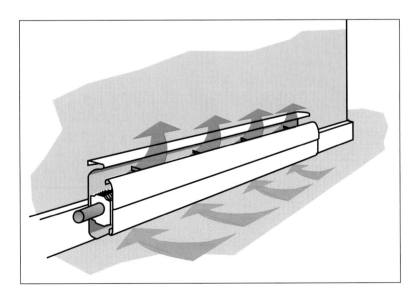

Figure 3.12 A fintube diffuser contains a series of closely spaced metal plates to increase the transfer of heat from the supply pipe to the air.

33

SUPPLEMENTAL HEATERS

So far, we've covered the most common ways to heat a house with a **central** system, which contains a heating device and means of distributing heat throughout the house. There are many products available that combine these features into a single unit. Some heat only one room, while others can heat a whole house if properly designed.

Stoves and Fireplaces

Stoves have evolved over the years and come in a wide variety of shapes, sizes and materials. They burn wood, coal, pellets, gas and even corn, all with greater efficiencies and less pollution than their predecessors. Glass-faced models display the flame, which adds aesthetic appeal. Except for unvented gas stoves, all require a flue for exhaust gasses and the clearances required between the walls and floors for a stove limit its possible locations in the house. A kitchen or bath presents an unlikely site for a stove.

Fireplaces are inadequate as heat sources. Anyone sitting in front of one feels the warm, comforting sensation of the flame, but the heat doesn't go much past that point. In fact, open fireplaces rob more heat from the house than they supply. There are, of course, ways to improve this balance. Glass doors enclosing the firebox will keep room air from being sucked up the flue. If they are added, there must also be a separate outside air supply to the firebox. Still, uncoupling the fire from the room robs the fireplace of some of its appeal, so many people still prefer the open fire—whatever the results. Fireplaces are popular in "country kitchens" and make a luxurious amenity for an upscale bath.

Gas fireplaces mimic the effect of burning wood, with fake logs that are constantly engulfed by the flames from the burner below. While the effect falls short of a real log burning, these units are much less demanding to operate. You simply turn them off and on. They come in vented and unvented models that need no flue. The gas appliance industry has largely addressed earlier concerns about the emissions of unvented gas stoves, specifically carbon monoxide. A national safety standard for vent-free gas appliances, ANSI Z21.11.2, requires vent-free products to satisfy numerous construction and performance requirements. The safety standard is approved by the American National Standard Institute (ANSI) and is developed by an independent committee comprised of representatives from various interests including state and federal regulatory authorities, utilities, manufacturers, consumers and general interests. Vent-free gas products are certified for compliance with this standard to assure their safety.

Unit Heaters

Unit heaters that mount next to an outside wall make good auxiliary heat sources for hard-to-heat areas such as a single-room addition. **Direct-vent heaters** draw combustion air into the fire chamber through a vent in the wall and exhaust the burnt gasses back out through another, concentric vent. Room air circulates around the fire chamber, never coming in contact with the combustion air. Gas-fired heating units and direct-vent heaters come in various heating capacities, from 12,000 Btu to around 35,000 Btu. There are also unvented heaters, which can be located anywhere in the room.

Heating products are constantly evolving and there are many variations to the systems mentioned above. Some heating devices are combined into cooling equipment, as we'll see in the next chapter.

Figure 3.13 A unit heater provides a way to heat an addition without altering the central heating system. The gas unit shown circulates warmed air around the heating chamber inside. Combustion air enters and exits through the wall without mixing with the room air.

CHAPTER 4: Cooling Systems

Human comfort is the goal of cooling, as well as heating systems. Referring back to the Human Comfort Zone, Figure 3.1, you can see that people feel comfortable when the dry bulb air temperature ranges between around 70° to 80°F (20°–27°C) when the relative humidity ranges between 20% and 70%. We can still feel warm at 45°F (10°C), if we are in the sun.

At the other end, we can still feel comfortable with temperatures as high as 90°F (32°C) if the air is moving. To succeed, cooling equipment must make us feel comfortable when the ambient conditions are outside of the comfort range of the chart.

COOLING NATURALLY

Cooling with mechanical means incurs costs. The first cost is that of the equipment and installation. Next comes the cost of operating the equipment over its expected lifetime, which includes the maintenance and fuels. Finally, there are less obvious, harder-to-measure costs to the environment, from extracting the fuels and polluting the air and water in converting the fuels into the energy that powers equipment to make us feel comfortable.

We can do much to minimize our dependence on mechanical cooling by constructing our homes intelligently and drawing upon natural energies when we can.

Not all natural cooling strategies work everywhere or all of the time. Savvy designers understand the climatic assets and limitations of their location and how to use them to **passively cool** homes. They bring on the big guns—mechanical devices that rely on purchased energy—only after they have exhausted the possibilities for simpler means. Even then, they start with the lowest-energy ones, such as fans and leave the most complicated and costly devices such as refrigerated air conditioning as a last resort.

Engineers call strategies that minimize the demand, or load, on cooling equipment **load avoidance**. Here are some of them.

Blocking Solar Heat

Windows contribute as much as one third of the total cooling season heat gain in homes in southern regions of the U.S. Most of this heat comes directly from solar radiation, rather than hot outside air coming into the house. It stands to reason that the first line of defense against overheating should be some means of blocking this sunshine. Trees do this elegantly. And deciduous trees even have the courtesy to drop their leaves in the winter when we would like the heat of the sun. Unfortunately, trees may not be available or in the right location. Roof overhangs and exterior shutters and shades can do the trick just as well (shades and blinds inside the house are less effective, since the heat of the sun has already penetrated through the window). Roof overhangs should be large enough to block solar heat when it isn't wanted but small enough to admit it in winter (for sizing overhangs, see NKBA's *Residential Construction* book).

Window films and low-emissivity (low-E) coated glass are also effective in keeping unwanted solar heat outside. Window films can be messy and unappealing, however, while low-E coating is invisible. Window manufacturers offer guidelines that tell which low-E coating is the most appropriate for the climate of a particular region.

Natural Ventilation

Air in motion serves two purposes in houses: maintaining indoor air quality and cooling. Ventilation promotes cooling directly or indirectly. When a breeze moves over your skin, it evaporates perspiration and removes latent heat, making you feel cooler. But if the conditions are above the comfort zone (see Figure 3.1), ventilation doesn't work. It can even make you feel hotter. **Direct ventilation** is effective means of cooling in the dry-bulb temperature range of 80–90°F (27–32°C), if the relative humidity stays below 80%. Fortunately, these conditions prevail in much of North America for all but the worst parts of summer, usually the last two weeks of July and first two weeks of August.

Regions with hot-dry climates, such as in the southwestern desert regions of the U.S., usually have large swings in temperature from day to night. Very hot days are often followed by cool or cold nights. Designers can exploit this feature to cool houses through **indirect ventilation**. Walls and floors made of dense concrete or masonry materials have excellent heat-storing capacities that allow them to absorb and release heat slowly. Simply opening windows at night to allow cool breezes to cool the massive walls and floors naturally cools the interior in much of the year. Closing the windows in the morning allows the cooled materials to absorb heat from the house.

Using Nature

Cross ventilation is one way we can take advantage of natural ventilation, by trapping the breezes that blow across the house. Windows on opposite walls of a room are the best way to flood the space with cooling that's free for the taking. But most rooms back up to other parts of the house rather than to an outside wall. Windows on adjacent walls are almost as effective if the windows are far enough apart to ensure a long path of any breeze entering. A room with windows on only one wall gets little ventilation unless a door on the opposite wall opens to a part of the house that creates a path for the breeze to traverse.

Casement and awning windows are better ventilators than double-hung or sliding windows for two reasons. First, they open outward and the protruding sash directs passing breezes into the room. Second, their entire sash opens, whereas only half of a double-hung or slider opens.

The stack effect provides another means of natural ventilation by exploiting the tendency of warm air to rise. Some traditional homes in the southern states had belvederes—roof towers with grilles—atop the center of their roofs. Air from open windows on the first floor would rise up in a central stairway and escaped through the belvedere, cooling the house in its wake. This strategy can be had in today's houses with operable skylights in the roof, a particular benefit to kitchens that have limited window area because cabinets take up much of the wall area.

Figure 4.1 A house designed to maximize natural ventilation contains openings situated to promote the flow of air through the entire structure. Southern houses, such as shown here, could serve as a model. Note the openings in the hallway walls and belvedere on the roof.

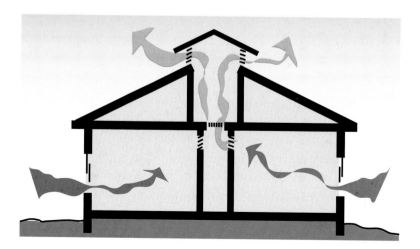

COOLING WITH FANS

Natural ventilation is easy and cheap when it's available. But wind is undependable. We can supplement natural ventilation by fans—separate fans in each room or a central fan capable of ventilating the whole house.

Ceiling fans can both cool a room and distribute the heat more evenly. They make the best sense in the larger rooms of the house with ceilings at least 8-feet (2,438 mm) high. Baths are not usually good candidates because of their smaller size and the need for a means of ventilation to ensure air quality, as we'll see in the next chapter. Much the same applies to kitchens, even though they may be larger. Ceiling fans require clearance of at least 10 inches (254 mm) between the ceiling and fan blades in order to provide adequate circulation. Guidelines for sizing ceiling fans are shown in the chart below.

Sizing Ceiling Fans	
Largest dimension of room	Minimum fan diameter
12 feet (3,658 mm) or less	36-inches (914 mm)
12 – 16 feet (3,658 – 4,877 mm)	48-inches (1,219 mm)
16 – 17.5 feet (4,877 – 5,334 mm)	52-inches (1,321 mm)
17.5 – 18.5 feet (5,334 – 5,639 mm)	56-inches (1,422 mm)
18.5 feet + (5,639 mm+)	2 fans

Figure 4.2 Ceiling fans provide a low-tech means for cooling through ventilation.

A **whole-house fan** pulls air in through windows opened at least 4 inches (102 mm) and exhausts it through vents in the attic. It cools the house by moving the air (direct ventilation) and by keeping the heat in the attic from building up. Whole-house fans should be sized to provide 20 air changes per hour (ach) to be effective. You can obtain the cubic feet per minute (cfm) rating required for this air change rate by multiplying the volume of the house by 0.33. The fan typically sits atop a grille in the upper floor ceiling and exhausts the air to the outside via vents in the gable ends of the attic, as shown in Figure 4.3.

Figure 4.3 Whole-house fans can be located in the gable end of the attic or attic floor (top); hot air may be exhausted through a belvedere on the roof (middle); or through vents in the gable end (bottom).

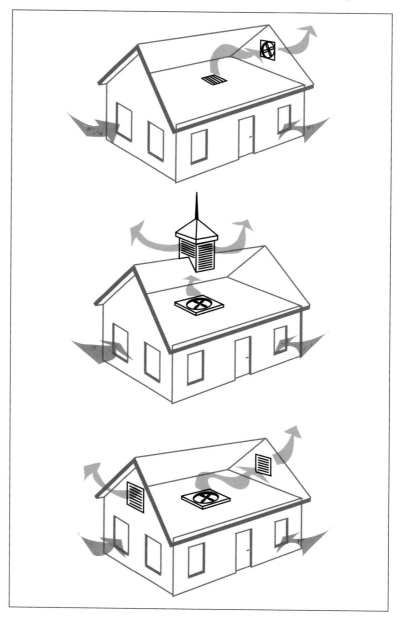

EVAPORATIVE COOLING

The same principle that cools your coffee can cool your house and do it more simply and economically than refrigeration equipment. As the name implies, evaporative cooling works by evaporating water into the airstream. In much the same way as the steam rising off a hot cup of coffee carries its heat away, when you put water in contact with incoming warm air, the water will evaporate into the air. When heat energy in the air changes the water from liquid to vapor, it cools the air in the process.

But there's a catch: evaporative cooling works best in climates that are both hot and dry. The most popular way to use evaporative cooling is with "swamp" coolers and they are widely used in the southwestern part of the U.S. How effective they are in lowering the temperature depends largely on how much moisture is already present in the air. The table below gives an idea of how much cooling to expect for various temperatures and humidity levels.

Cooling Potential of Evaporative Cooling		
Dry Bulb Temperature	Relative Humidity	Number of degrees temperature can be lowered
75° (24°C)	70 to 80%	3 to 4°F
80°F (27°C)	50 to 60%	6 to 9°F
85°F (29°C)	30 to 55%	10 to 15°F
90°F (32°C)	20 to 30%	16 to 20°F
95°F (35°C)	10 to 20%	21 to 25°F
100°F (38°C)	5 to 10%	27 to 29°F
105°F (41°C)	2 to 5%	31 to 33°F
110°F (43°C)	2%	35°F

Evaporative cooling is more complicated and costs more than natural ventilation, but far less than refrigeration cooling (air conditioning). Homes in regions that favor evaporative cooling can enjoy these advantages over refrigerated systems:

- Lower initial cost

- Lower peak energy usage

- Lower operating cost

- Less greenhouse gas production

- No CFC's or HFC's, hence no depletion of the ozone in the atmosphere

- The cooled air is more humid. Refrigerated systems can dehydrate the air too much on a dry day

- Constantly floods the house with fresh air

- The wet filter pads filter the air

- Occupants don't have to worry about windows or doors being left open

Evaporative coolers typically mount on the roof, though through-wall units are also available. There are two types of systems, **direct** and **indirect**.

Direct Evaporative Cooling

This system is the most widely used in the areas of the southwest. A large fan takes in huge amounts of hot outside air and blows it into the house through a pad, or filter, kept constantly moist by recirculated and make-up water. The effect on the occupants is a gently moving stream of cooler air.

Indirect Evaporative Cooling

Because direct evaporative cooling adds moisture to the air, it does not suit hot humid regions. However, an indirect evaporative system gets around this hurdle by isolating the moist, cooled air from the room air. It does this by passing the cooled air through an assembly of finned coils, around which the room air circulates.

Both types of coolers mount on the roof, with a small-diameter pipe to supply make-up water and another to drain it to the ground. Through-wall units are also available.

Figure 4.4 Direct evaporative coolers pull hot outside air through a wetted pad and deliver cooled air to the interior. This method works best in the hot-dry climates of the U.S. Southwest.

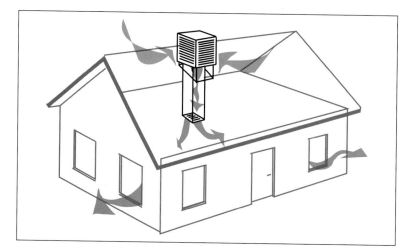

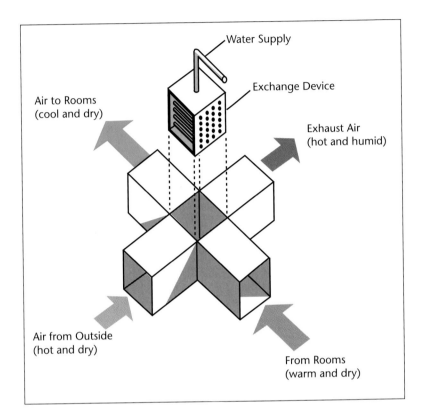

Water Supply

Exchange Device

Air to Rooms
(cool and dry)

Exhaust Air
(hot and humid)

Air from Outside
(hot and dry)

From Rooms
(warm and dry)

Figure 4.5 Indirect evaporative coolers do not mix the air cooled by evaporation with the air supplied to the interior. This feature makes them viable for regions that have more humid air.

REFRIGERATION COOLING

Reliance on the simplest, least polluting technologies and energy sources benefits everyone. That's why we began discussing cooling by describing passive cooling techniques such as natural ventilation and solar heat avoidance, then went on to cooling systems that use some outside energy, such as fans and evaporative coolers. We left the most complicated and energy-consuming devices that rely on refrigeration cooling until last, because they should be the last resort when simpler means fail. Unfortunately, passive and low-energy devices have their limits. In areas where **high temperatures combine with high humidity** for much of the year, refrigeration devices are the only means of making a house comfortable. The region most dependent on refrigeration cooling for at least part of the year includes the southeastern and mid-Atlantic regions of the U.S. Southern Florida relies on this type of cooling year-round.

Refrigeration cooling (also called air conditioning or mechanical cooling) gets its name from the same process that cools the air in your refrigerator. In simplest form it works like this: A compressor compresses gas at room temperature. As it is compressed it becomes

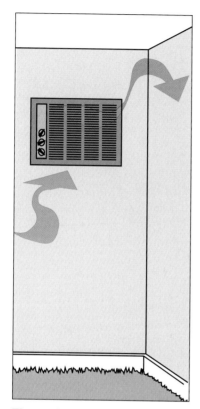

Figure 4.6 Room air conditioners are effective in areas where extreme temperature and humidity levels are a concern. Mounting them high on the wall, as shown here, is more effective than placing them in a low window opening.

hot. It flows in a compressed state through a coil to cool it back to room temperature. Then it releases through a nozzle into the coil inside the refrigerator. As the pressure diminishes, the gas cools, but *below the* room temperature. Bingo, cooled air on your food. The process cools building interiors by various types of systems. Some even combine heating capability.

Room Air Conditioners

Devices that contain the refrigeration and distribution equipment in a single unit are called room air conditioners. With this method the distribution system consists of a fan that delivers cooled air at various speeds to the room. While mounting a room air conditioner in the lower portion of a window opening is easy and convenient, it does not cool a room as efficiently as placing the air conditioner in a special opening high in the wall, since cool air tends to sink to the floor. Besides, an air conditioner in a window blocks out light from that portion and means the window cannot be opened on a cool day.

Room air conditioners come in various sizes and cooling capacities from 5,000 to 29,000 Btu. Bigger is not better when sizing an air conditioner. An oversized unit cycles on and off less frequently, producing greater swings in temperature and humidity than a smaller unit that cycles on and off more often. In general, a well-insulated room requires from 20 to 40 Btu per square foot of area to be cooled. Electricity is the usual fuel source for a room air conditioner and units can work off either a 120v or 220v power source. Those wired to 220v power get better efficiency, but a separate 220v outlet must be provided.

Central Air Conditioning

When cooling the whole house is the goal, a central system is the answer. There are two main configurations, a **split-system** and a **ducted system**. Both divide the task of cooling the air from the means of delivering it to the rooms.

In a **split-system**, the compressor sits on a concrete pad outside the house, connected to fan-coil units in the walls of various rooms. Small-diameter copper piping provides the umbilical cord between the unit and fan-coils mounted in walls or ceilings of the rooms. Fans deliver cooled air from the coils to the rooms. In addition to cooling the whole house, split-systems have another advantage over individual room units—less noise. With the compressor unit outside, the only noise the occupants hear is the sound of the fan.

Ducted System

The duct network that delivers warm air in winter can do double duty in the summer in a **ducted air conditioning system**, but with a trade-off. Because warm air rises, the best place to run ducts for heating is below the floor of the rooms to be heated. Just the opposite is true of cooling, so using below-floor ducts for a ducted air conditioning system isn't as efficient as mounting them in the ceiling. This can be done, of course, in regions that need little or no heat in winter. Small kitchens present a special problem, since they probably have little if any free wall space and floor-mounted diffusers are impractical in kitchens. Whereas heating can be delivered through a toe-space diffuser under a cabinet, cold air squeezed through a narrow aperture this close to the floor will result in little other than cold feet. If you face this situation, try to find a location high on a wall for the diffuser.

Like split-systems, ducted systems are quieter than individual room air conditioners. Compared to split-systems, ducting is trickier to run and eats up more space than refrigeration piping. On the other hand, ducted systems can use the same ducts used by the forced-air heating, if one is willing to accept some compromise in efficiency.

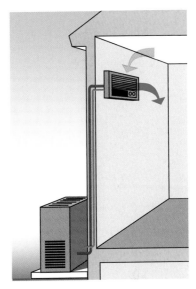

Figure 4.7 (above) In a split air conditioning system the compressor is located outdoors and is connected by piping to fan-coil diffusers in the walls of the rooms.

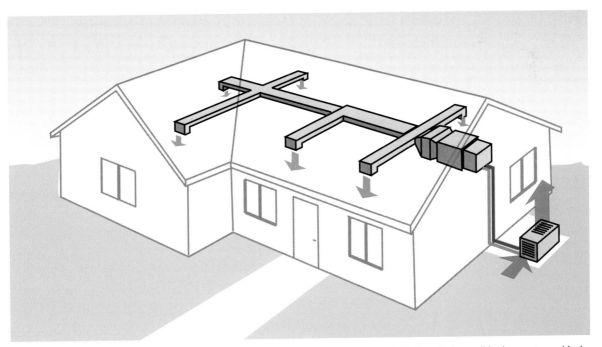

Figure 4.8 (above) A ducted air conditioning system with the ducts overhead is the best choice for cooling-only systems. When the need for heating dominates, ducts are usually run in the floor.

RATING THE EFFICIENCY OF REFRIGERATED COOLING

Refrigerated cooling requires more electrical energy than passive or low-energy means, so homeowners will naturally want the most efficient equipment. Efficiency in a general sense is the output divided by the input, such as miles per gallon in vehicles. We use two measures to rate the efficiency of refrigeration devices.

The **energy efficiency rating (EER)** measures the efficiency of room air conditioners. The EER is the ratio of the cooling output in Btu divided by the power consumption in kilowatt-hours. A room air conditioner with an EER of 9.5 is considered efficient. Each unit bears a label stating its EER.

Central air conditioners and heat pumps operating in the cooling mode are rated by their performance over the cooling season. The **seasonal energy efficiency rating (SEER)** is obtained by dividing the cooling output in Btu by the energy in kilowatt-hours required to operate the equipment in the cooling season in an average U.S. climate. A SEER of 10 was established in 1992 as the national appliance efficiency standard for central air conditioners.

Central air conditioners almost always beat out room units in energy efficiency. Features that can help make them operate efficiently include:

- A fan-only switch to allow ventilation only.

- A filter check light that comes on when the predetermined life time of the filter is exhausted.

- An automatic delay fan switch to turn the fan off a few minutes after the compressor turns off.

HEAT PUMPS – COMBINING HEATING WITH COOLING

If air conditioners are basically refrigerators that pump heat out of the house, why couldn't we just turn them around in winter to pump heat back inside? We can and do with a device that works much like an air conditioner that can move heat in either direction. Using the same principle as a refrigeration air conditioner, a heat pump extracts heat from a space at low temperature and discharges it to another space at higher temperature.

The system consists of two heat exchangers, a compressor and expansion valve and interconnecting piping filled with a refrigerant. Electricity powers the compressor. By reversing the direction of the refrigerant flow with a valve, the system can be used to either heat or cool.

Heat pumps work well in houses in climates that need both heating and cooling, which includes much of the continental U.S. and southern Canada. They are not likely to be the most cost-effective choice for climates that seldom or never need refrigeration cooling. Heat pumps are available in three configurations.

Single-Room Heat Pumps

Single-Room Heat Pumps are basically room air conditioners equipped to reverse the cycle. A single-room heat pump delivers heat efficiently when outside temperatures are above 45°F (7°C). When temperatures drop lower than this, efficiency falls off until the unit produces too little heat to be useful in the heat pump mode. It then shifts the heating task onto a back-up resistance heating coil to make up the deficit. This, of course, makes it a costly heating source in regions with cold winters and high costs for electricity. You can get an idea of whether a single-room heat pump is cost-effective for your region from manufacturers' published data, specifically the *heating seasonal performance factor* (HSPF.) The HSPF equals the total annual heating output in Btu divided by the total electrical output in watt-hours during the heating season.

Split-System Heat Pumps

Split-System Heat Pumps heat and cool more than one room by separating the compressor from the distribution system. The system uses much the same configuration as a split-system air conditioning system. An outside-mounted compressor feeds chilled refrigerant to fan-coil units in the rooms. A fan blows through the coil to heat or cool the room. As with single-room heat pumps, this type heats efficiently only when outside temperatures are above 45°F (7°C), below which they switch over to heating via an electric resistance element in the fan coil.

Ducted Systems

Ducted Systems resemble central or whole-house air conditioning in their configuration, with the heat pump unit mounted outside and cooled air distributed to the rooms through ducts. Ducted heat pump systems incur the same tradeoffs as ducted heating systems, in that overhead ducts work best for cooling, while below-floor ducts excel for heating. The best location for ducts depends on the type of structure (a single level house on a concrete slab has only one possible location, the ceiling) and relative demand for heating vs. cooling.

Heat pumps also vary according to the medium they use to extract heat. Most heat pumps today use the air as their heat exchange medium and are called **air-to-air** heat pumps. Another type has gained popularity in recent years. A **ground-coupled heat pump (GCHP)** uses the warmth or coolness of the ground to heat or cool a house.

Because ground temperatures are more stable than air temperatures, GCHPs aren't as sensitive to daily and seasonal swings in temperature as air-to-air systems. GCHPs circulate a heat transfer fluid between the heat pump unit through a buried piping loop that absorbs the earth's natural warmth in winter and rejects heat to the earth in summer.

A second type, a **groundwater heat pump (GWHP)** draws water from a well or pond, exchanges the heat with a refrigerant, then discharges the water into a rejection well, disposal pond or storm sewer. This approach is obviously limited to houses close to a water source.

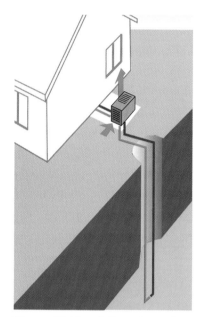

Figure 4.9 (above) Groundwater heat pumps extract heating or cooling from water by piping extending vertically into a pond or well.

Figure 4.10 (right) Because the ground is warmer than the air in winter and cooler in summer it can be utilized for heating or cooling in-ground-coupled heat pumps. Water circulates through piping buried in the yard, extracting heat from the ground in winter and expelling heat into the ground during the cooling season.

CHAPTER 5: Maintaining Healthy Indoor Air

The trend toward greater energy efficiency in homes means homes are sealed up against cold drafts. There is, unfortunately, a downside to tight houses. By sealing them up to keep cold drafts at bay we also shut down the fresh air that would otherwise cleanse the interior of contaminants. The gasses and particles that pollute the rooms of our houses have many sources: smoking, burning wood in stoves, operating unvented gas appliances, bathing and cooking, to name a few. Chemicals used for cleaning are other sources. But some indoor air pollution comes from items the occupants have no control over. Formaldehyde and organic chemicals used in the manufacture of carpeting and building materials gradually release (outgas) to the air in the room.

Some of the culprits that contaminate the air of our houses are not necessarily unhealthy, simply objectionable. Odors produced in the kitchen and bathroom fall into this category. Others, such as second-hand smoke from cigarettes, are definite health hazards. Regardless of the contaminant, the occupants will be healthier and happier if it is removed to the outside.

THE SOURCES OF INDOOR AIR POLLUTION

The culprits that contaminate indoor air are many and varied in their potential for damaging health and well being. Here are some of the major offenders and means of eliminating or reducing them in homes.

Radon, a colorless, odorless gas, is a radioactive product of the radium that naturally occurs in the earth's crust. Radon poses a risk to people in regions with high concentrations of certain types of rock strata. It is believed responsible for 5 to 15 percent of all lung cancer. Radon gas seeps into houses through miniscule cracks in foundations and basement floors and can also occur in water from wells.

Preventing radon from getting into a house is easier at the construction stage than after it is built. Special care can seal up cracks in the floors and walls. Foundations can be waterproofed on the outside. A gravel bed below the basement slab can act as a continuous evacuation path to the outside when it is equipped with a fan that pulls air through the gravel and exhausts it outside. The homeowner has few means available to mitigate radon in an existing home short of sealing up visible cracks in the foundation and basement slab and installing a ventilation system in the basement.

Formaldehyde is a strong-smelling yet colorless gas embodied in many common building materials, such as plywood and particleboard, as well as furniture, drapes and carpets made from synthetic materials. This gas can irritate the nose, throat and eyes and may case nasal cancer. Materials that contain little or no formaldehyde should be chosen at the outset. Increasing the rate of air changes in the house helps, after the fact.

Combustion Gasses. Several noxious gasses come from operating kerosene heaters, wood stoves and unvented gas appliances. Car exhaust in attached garages can also seep into the house through doorways. Deadly in high enough concentrations, carbon monoxide is a colorless, odorless, tasteless gas produced by burning all fuels. In lesser concentrations this gas can impair the lungs, eyes and brain. Nitrogen oxide has no color or odor while nitrogen dioxide does have an odor at higher levels. Long exposure to either can cause lung damage.

Mitigating pollution from combustion appliances begins at the device. Wood stoves should be properly sized and vented. Appliances should be adjusted correctly. Outside air into wood stoves and fireplaces is preferred to using room air. Chimneys need to be kept clean. A car should never be left idling in the garage.

Particulates. Smoking releases particles into the air small enough to be inhaled. Minor exposure may result in irritation to the eyes and respiratory system. Long-term exposure can cause emphysema, heart disease, bronchitis and lung cancer. Other sources of particulates include unvented gas appliances, kerosene heaters, asbestos-bearing construction materials and dust. Solutions include not smoking inside, making sure oven doors don't leak, changing air filters regularly and providing an outside air source for combustion appliances.

Gasses from Household Chemicals. Many organic compounds found in cleaning agents, pesticides, aerosol sprays, paints and solvents can irritate the eyes, skin, nose, throat and central nervous system. Some household chemicals are available in "green" versions that do not harm health. Latex paints, for example, use water as their solvent, rather than solvents derived from petroleum. Other remedies include following the directions on the label, using chemicals only in well-ventilated areas and keeping them locked away from children.

You may have noticed that ventilation, in one form or another, is mentioned as a remedy for all of the indoor air pollutants. A grasp of the techniques and devices that provide ventilation will help you achieve clean, healthy indoor air for your clients.

MOISTURE

Moisture, or water vapor, while not a noxious gas, can jeopardize the health of the occupants, as well as the structure. For these reasons, moisture levels can't be ignored when we are talking about indoor air quality.

We can't live in a house without producing moisture. For starters we add moisture to the air every time we perspire or take a breath. We dump large amounts of moisture into the air while showering, bathing, boiling water or cooking food. Substantial moisture may enter the house apart from anything the occupants do. A house constructed without proper vapor barriers can fall prey to moisture seeping into basements through masonry walls or wicking up through the soil below a crawl space.

We need some moisture in the air to maintain a healthy respiratory system and to keep our skin from becoming too dry. Most people feel comfortable when the air they inhale contains between 40 and 60 percent relative humidity. Continuous moisture above these levels, however, can be a health hazard by promoting the growth of microorganisms and acting as a solvent for other pollutants.

Excessive moisture can also damage the house. When the indoor temperature is higher than the one outdoors, the warm air inside seeks to find a path out (Remember from the discussion of heat in Chapter 3 that heat travels from a warmer to colder location.). As the warm air wends its way through the cracks and crannies of the structure, it meets a point in the structure, the dew point, where the dry- and wet-bulb temperatures coincide. Moisture in the air condenses and collects on building materials, where it can rot framing and wall sheathing, peel exterior paint and create ice dams on the eaves.

The means of controlling moisture begin at the drawing phase of a project and continue through the proper installation of vapor barriers, insulation, exhaust fans, etc., by installers. The occupants then assume the responsibility and can control excess indoor moisture buildup by heeding the following advice:

- Don't intentionally add moisture by leaving a kettle boiling on a wood stove.

- Don't store green firewood in the heated part of the house.

51

- Duct clothes dryers to the outside, never into an attic or basement.

- Use a ducted exhaust fan when cooking.

- Use a ducted exhaust fan when bathing or showering.

The lion's share of indoor moisture in a home is generated in the kitchen and bath—your area of specialization. As a kitchen and bath designer you can do your part by properly designing moisture control devices for rooms under your responsibility and getting involved with the client and the building team early on to communicate the problems and solutions relating to moisture control.

FRESH AIR THROUGH VENTILATION

We saw in the last chapter how ventilation, whether natural or fan-forced, can help in cooling a house. Ventilation is also needed to ensure good air quality by evacuating contaminated air to the outside and replacing it with cleaner outside air. (Unfortunately, there are times in the summer when the outside air in many large urban areas has high levels of ozone and other contaminants, making it an unhealthy make-up source). Obtaining fresh air in mild weather is as easy as opening a window. It presented no challenge in older houses, even in cold weather. Enough fresh air leaked in through cracks around windows and doors to maintain a supply of fresh air to the interior. These paths were blocked when houses were sealed up to achieve better energy efficiency. The most energy-efficient houses built today rely on mechanical means to provide the necessary air changes.

The exact amount of fresh air required is measured in **air changes per hour (ach)**—the number times all of the air in the house is replaced with outside air. The American Society of Heating, Refrigeration and Air Conditioning Engineers (ASHRAE) recommends a minimum ach of 0.35 to maintain healthy air inside the house. To put this number into perspective, a well-sealed new home gets up to 0.6 ach and a reasonably tight older home gets around 1.0 ach. Fairly loose, drafty, homes get air changes of 4 ach or greater.

The *Canadian National Building Code* lists the requirements for ventilation according to the season. Ventilation during the non-heating season can come from natural or mechanical sources. If the room is mechanically cooled, the equipment must provide a minimum of 0.5 ach. Bathrooms are required to have openable ventilation areas (the area of an opened window, for example) of at least 0.09 m². Other living areas must have a minimum of 0.28 m².

The Canadian code specifies that every dwelling supplied with electrical power must have mechanical ventilation system for the heating season. Ventilating capacities are specified by volume of air per second in liters/second (L/s) rather than air changes per hour. Ventilating equipment for kitchens and baths must provide at least 5 L/s.

There are many ways to bring in air from the outside through mechanical ventilation. All depend on electrically operated fans, acting on their own or coupled with other mechanical equipment. We'll scan some of the main options, from the simplest to most complex.

VENTILATING ROOM BY ROOM

Spot ventilation removes moisture, odors and pollutants directly at the source. Here are some of the most common devices that use this approach.

Room Exhaust Fans

The simplest, most economical way to move stale air out and fresh air into a room is to install a ducted exhaust fan on an outside wall or in the ceiling. Codes state the requirements for mechanical ventilation for baths that don't have direct access to outside air via a window or other opening.

The exhaust capacity depends on the size of the room. You can determine the proper capacity by dividing the volume of the room in cubic feet by 7.5. For example, a bath measuring 8 feet by 12 feet with a ceiling height of 8 feet has a volume of 768 cubic feet (length x width x height). An adequately sized exhaust fan for this room is:

$$768 \div 7.5 = 102 \text{ cfm.}$$

Capacities of fans currently available range between 75 and 600 cfm, so finding one that could handle this room would be relatively easy. Fan flow ratings are based on an assumed resistance to airflow. If you are designing an installation with a duct run longer than 5 feet (1,524 mm) or with more than one elbow, plan on upsizing the fan capacity higher than that you'll obtain from the formula above.

The chief drawback of individual exhaust fans is their noise. Fans produce noise by themselves and when mounted into a ceiling can vibrate the ceiling board to add to the overall noise. Fan noise is measured in units called sones. The quietest kitchen and bath exhaust fans produce around 1 sone, about the same noise as a refrigerator fan. The noisiest ones yield up to 4 sones. The noise plus inconvenience of having to remember to turn them on and off are probably why exhaust fans don't get used as much as they ought to. The Home Ventilating Institute suggests that timers be connected to bath exhaust fans. They should be set for the shower time plus 20 minutes to ensure all moist air is evacuated.

Figure 5.1 Room exhaust fans can mount in walls or ceilings. Ducting, when necessary, should be as short and direct as possible.

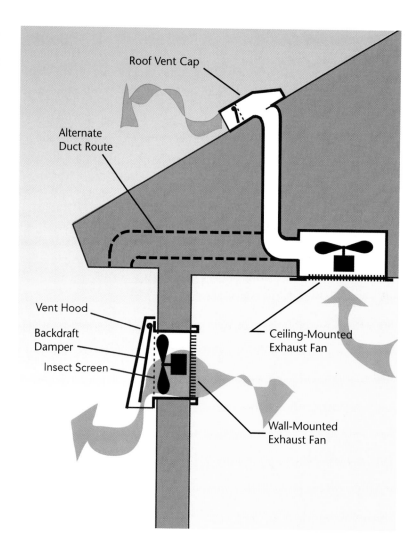

Kitchen Exhaust Devices

The aroma of bread baking in the oven or a hearty soup steaming on the stove on a cold winter day evokes warm feelings. But cooking also pollutes the air with grease, smoke, undesirable odors, moisture and even some toxic emissions from gas ranges, making it the major source of air pollution in most homes today. The most effective way to remove these gasses is at the source—the cooktop or range. Exhaust can be removed from either above, or at, the cooking surface.

Range hoods, vent hoods and shrouds capture heated gasses as they rise off the cooking surface. Inside the hood a fan pulls the hot gasses through a filter to trap grease and evacuate the gasses through a duct to the outside. Recirculating, or unvented, models that don't require ducts are also available. They merely pull air through the filter and return it to the room. Because they can't remove combustion gasses, they are not as effective as ducted units and should only be used in cases where it is impossible to duct the exhaust to the outside.

Manufacturers offer range hoods in several sizes, capacities and designs. Many incorporate fans and lights. Off-the-shelf models come in widths of 24-, 30-, 36-, 42- and 48-inches wide to match the widths of the ranges they serve. Some kitchen designers suggest that the range hood will perform more effectively if it is wider than the range by one size.

Figure 5.2 Recirculating range hoods return filtered air to the room and should be used only in cases where it is impossible to provide a vented model, which expels exhaust gasses to the outside.

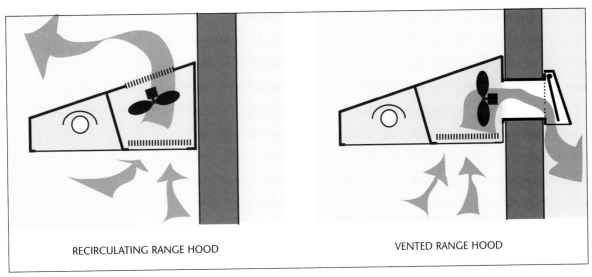

RECIRCULATING RANGE HOOD   VENTED RANGE HOOD

Figure 5.3 Typical range hood installation. Note that for best performance, the hood is wider than the range.

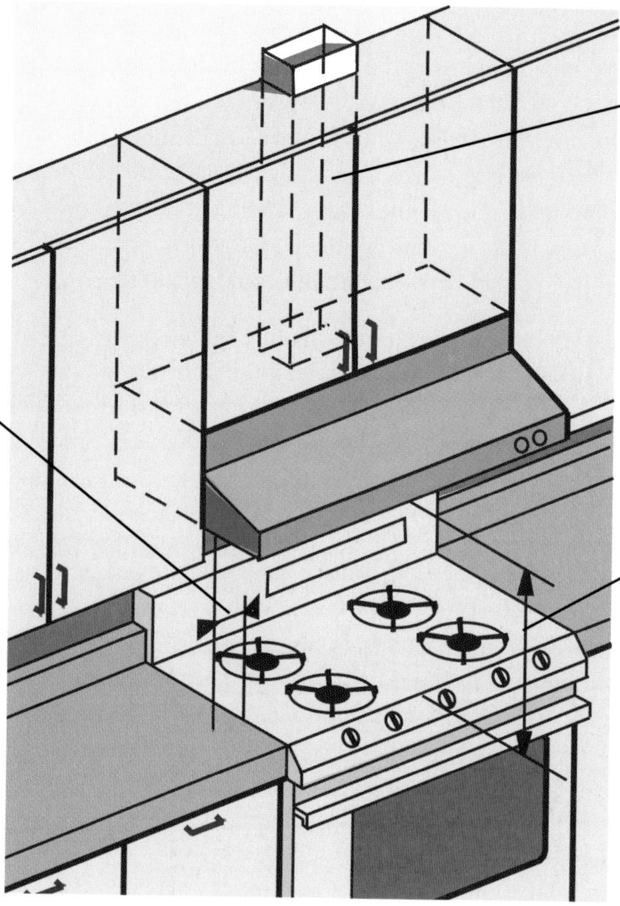

Duct to exhaust through roof or rear wall

3" (36 mm) wider than cooking surface

Height specified by manufacturer, typically 24" (610 mm)

As kitchens have become more than a utilitarian place to cook food, so has the equipment. The 30-inch wide range that served past generations so well no longer satisfies many homeowners today. They look to larger models incorporating features of professional-style ranges.

If you are designing a kitchen for this type of range or cooktop, you may be better served by choosing a high-powered professional-style hood, rather than an off-the-shelf range hood. Custom range hoods made of stainless steel or copper increasingly grace upscale kitchens.

Whatever the size and appearance of a range hood, it must be shaped and sized to effectively exhaust gasses from the cooking surface. The most effective hood shape looks something like an inverted bowl. The distance between the hood and cooking surface is also important. The hood should mount at a minimum of 24 inches (610 mm) above the range, but use the manufacturer's specifications to make the final determination.

Microwave ovens can do double duty as both cooking appliance and venting device for the range if it's mounted above the range. Vented models are preferred for this application over unvented (recirculating) ones, for reasons stated previously. As with vented range hoods, they take in exhaust gasses through a filter below the unit and expel them out the top or rear into a duct.

Figure 5.4 Microwave ovens mounted above the range can do double duty as both cooking and venting appliance. A recirculating model is shown here, however models that vent to the outside are preferred.

Vented (downdraft) ranges offer an alternative to overhead venting by incorporating an exhaust fan into the range itself. A fan below the cooking surface draws off foul air into a telescoping vent at the rear of the range or a grill in the cooking surface. Ducting routs through an adjacent outside wall or down through the floor and out through a basement wall. There seems to be no general consensus as to how vented ranges compare to overhead range hoods, except that they don't do as well for cooking with tall pots.

Figure 5.5 (right) Vented ranges can exhaust through a rear wall or downward under the floor. Ducting should be short and direct.

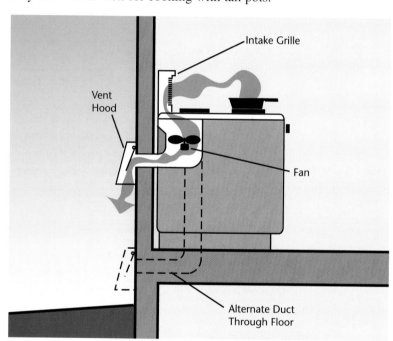

Figure 5.6 (below) Vented ranges contain fans that exhaust cooking gasses either through the deck or a pop-up vertical panel, which is more effective.

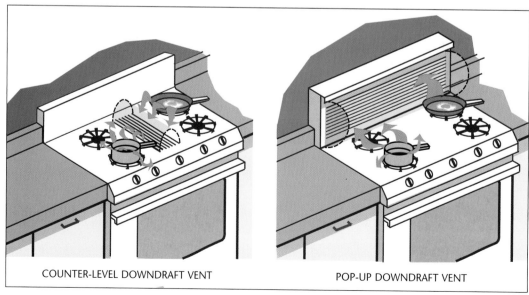

COUNTER-LEVEL DOWNDRAFT VENT   POP-UP DOWNDRAFT VENT

SIZING KITCHEN EXHAUST FANS

Devices that evacuate stale air above cooking surfaces come in varying capacities, according to the type of device. Too much is better than too little capacity.

Typical Airflow Rates of Range Exhaust Systems	
Range Hood	150 – 600 cfm
Island Hood	400 – 600 cfm
Microwave Hood	200 – 400 cfm
Downdraft Exhaust Fan	300 – 500 cfm

The NKBA recommends that the designer always check with the manufacturer of the cooktop or range for their cfm recommendation.

The minimum capacity that meets the current ASHRAE standard (ASHRAE 62-99) is 100 cfm. Number crunching aside, the safest approach is to give the client flexibility—with variable speed fans with enough maximum capacity to ensure adequate ventilation even when several pots are boiling at the same time. Most off-the-shelf range hoods contain a fan. When custom-designing a hood, you have the possibility of locating the fan in the duct (in-line fan) for quieter operation.

Range hoods connect to ducting either through the back or top. The duct can run through the ceiling, above the cabinets, or—if necessary—through cabinets to an exit on an outside wall or the roof. They terminate in a wall or roof vent kit that contains a shield to prevent water entry and a flapper that opens to allow exhaust air to escape but flaps shut when wind hits it. On windy days, the sound of the flapper can travel through the ducting to create an annoying noise in the house.

THE DANGER OF BACKDRAFTING

Exhaust fans expel air out of the home without supplying replacement, or make-up, air. In poorly sealed houses enough air might be drawn back in through cracks around windows and doors to make up the difference. But the lack of make-up air in tight houses can depressurize the house and suck air out of combustion appliances. The result of this "backdrafting" can be dangerous buildups of carbon monoxide (CO) and other noxious gasses. Gas water heater pilot lights and even supposedly airtight wood stoves with outside combustion air can malfunction with only slight negative room-air pressures. Here are some ways to avoid the hazard of backdrafting in tight homes:

- Provide a dedicated source of make-up air for the rooms.

- Use only sealed-combustion appliances (appliances that have a ducted supply of combustion air rather than drawing room air into the combustion chamber).

- Use several smaller exhaust fans rather than one large exhaust fan.

- Equip the home with one or more CO detector.

59

An Effective Ductwork System

A well-chosen or well-designed exhaust fan only gets you past the starting gate. The rest of the challenge is to ensure that the ductwork can carry the exhaust gasses to the exterior. Aim for the shortest, straightest path from the fan to the exterior. End the system with a wall termination kit or roof jack. Make sure all joints are tight and taped with pressure-sensitive tape that will last after the walls are enclosed. Other good advice:

- Specify galvanized steel, 28-gauge minimum.

- Specify rigid sheet duct material. If you must use a flexible material specify aluminum, but never plastic-based ducting.

- Provide a backdraft damper at the outlet of the duct.

- Specify a small mesh screen at the outlet of the duct to keep out birds and rodents.

- Make sure the fan is accessible for cleaning and servicing.

- Insulate ducts and other parts of the system where they come closer than 6 inches (152 mm) to wood framing or other combustible materials.

- Insulate ducts that pass through unheated spaces and insulate all duct runs for a distance of 36 inches (914 mm) from the point of exit.

- Don't use more than three 90-degree elbows.

- Don't locate elbows closer than 1 foot (305 mm) to each other to avoid eddies.

Round ducts move air more efficiently than rectangular ones, however it is not always possible to fit a round duct of the required diameter through the allotted space. Size ducts according to the following guidelines:

Fan located in ceiling, range hood, or downdraft range: 6 inch round or 3" x 10" rectangular, for a maximum duct length of 25 feet (7,620 mm).

Fan located inside the duct (in-line fan): 9 inch round or 3" x 10" rectangular, for a maximum duct length of 55 feet (16,764 mm).

For questions that may arise for specific application, consult the hood or appliance manufacturer.

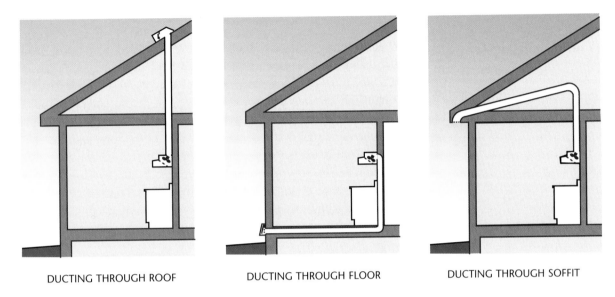

DUCTING THROUGH ROOF DUCTING THROUGH FLOOR DUCTING THROUGH SOFFIT

Figure 5.7 (above) The best route for exhaust ductwork is the shortest path with the fewest turns. The location of the fan in the house is the starting point, but the structure has to be considered. For example, ducting through the floor is possible only if the joists run parallel to the ducts. If not, the duct must run below the joists.

WHOLE-HOUSE VENTILATION SYSTEMS

Another way to get rid of stale indoor air is with a centrally located device. By whole-house ventilation we don't mean ventilation for cooling, as discussed earlier, but ventilation to ensure good air quality.

To begin, note that all room-by-room ventilation approaches have two things in common:

- Each contains its own fan.

- Each exhausts stale air but does not supply fresh air.

Both of these features have their downsides. A fan in a range hood or bathroom ceiling is close enough to the user to be heard and the noise of even a relatively quiet range hood can be annoying when the fan is operating at maximum speed. And expelling stale air without supplying replacement, or make-up, air depressurizes the interior, with the adverse effects we stated earlier. Whole-house ventilation systems address both of these concerns.

Multi-Point Fan Systems

Individual exhaust devices are typically installed in kitchens, baths and laundries—the rooms that generate most of the polluting gasses and moisture. Replacing the individual fans in these devices with a central fan at some distance from the point of use solves the noise problem. Systems of this type typically locate an "in-line" fan in a duct near the point of exit through an outer wall or the roof. Branch ducts below the fan extend to a grille in the ceiling of each room to be served. The fans run continuously at low speed with provision for high exhaust rates on an intermittent basis. Be sure to coordinate the in-line fan with the device served. A professional size range may need a fan capacity larger than may be available from the in-line fan.

Fresh air for houses with forced-air heating/cooling systems enters centrally into the return ducting near the furnace. In houses not heated or cooled by forced-air systems, inlet devices installed in outside walls admit the necessary make-up air. These inlets contain regulators to assure proper airflows at each grille. Inlets are mounted high on a wall to allow the un-tempered, cold air they bring in to mix with the warm air near the ceiling, so that it is comfortable by the time it reaches the level of the occupants.

Figure 5.8 A whole-house ventilation system can be integrated with a forced-air heating system by combining one or more exhaust fans with a fresh air intake to the furnace fan.

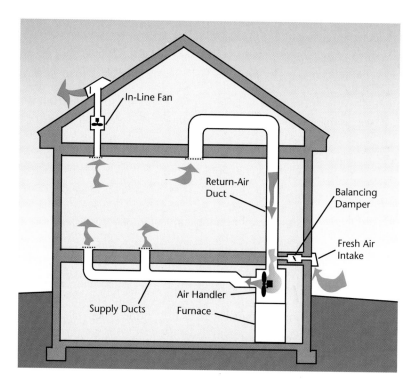

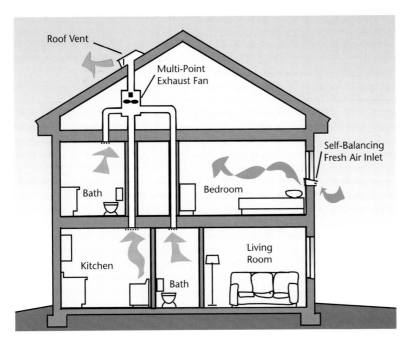

Figure 5.9 In a multi-point ventilation system there are no individual kitchen and bath exhaust fans. Instead, grilles in these rooms duct stale air to a central exhaust fan, usually in the attic. Make-up fresh air is introduced through self-balancing air inlets in the walls.

Heat Recovery Systems

Central fan systems properly designed to balance exhausted air with an equal amount of fresh air are excellent means of ensuring clean, healthy indoor air in a home. They fall short in one respect, however. The heat contained in the air expelled to the outside is wasted, along with the polluting gasses. Homeowners who invested money to make their homes energy efficient don't welcome the idea of blowing air that they paid to heat back outside.

Another type of central ventilation system addresses this issue by recovering much of the heat contained in the exhaust gasses, thereby saving the homeowner money on heating fuels. A **heat recovery ventilator (HRV)**, also know as an **air-to-air heat exchanger**, is basically a heat exchanger with two fans inside a metal box. One fan drives stale air out through one channel while another fan sucks fresh outside air in through a second, separate channel. Some of the heat from out-going air conducts through the metal that keeps the airstreams separate to warm the incoming air. Between 50 and 85 percent of the heat from out-going air is thus recovered in the fresh air. HRVs cost more than exhaust-only systems, but recoup the initial cost over time through savings on heating fuel. They are more cost-effective in cold climate regions such as the northern tier states of the U.S. and Canada than in more temperate southern regions and are not common in cooling-dominated regions.

HRVs are intended to maintain the air quality of the whole house and as so, to supplement, rather than replace, point-source exhaust fans above ranges and showers. HRVs mount in either the attic or basement. Whole-house systems require two distinct duct systems, one for supply air and one for return air. Ducts are smaller in diameter than those of a forced-air heating system and may be made of round rigid plastic, round flexible plastic, round sheet metal and rectangular sheet metal, according to which materials are accepted by the local building authority. Ducts run between the HRV unit and pick-up points located high on walls of living areas. An HRV unit is typically controlled by a 24-hour timer or runs continuously. Some have more than one speed and most can defrost to keep the transfer plates in the unit from frosting up in winter. After installation, the airflow in the system should be adjusted by the installer for proper balance and to prevent under- or over-ventilating.

Figure 5.10 A heat recovery ventilator (HRV) supplies fresh air to the interior and exhausts stale air to the outdoors. Coils inside the unit capture some of the heat from exhaust air indirectly to warm incoming fresh air.

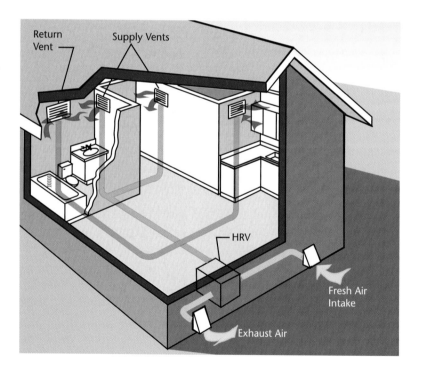

PART THREE: PLUMBING SYSTEMS

We're used to thinking of the rooms of a house in terms of their function. Seen in this light, kitchens and baths have different functions from other rooms in the house, even as kitchens are evolving toward becoming social centers, in addition to their traditional function as sites for food preparation. Baths, meanwhile, now serve needs that transcend their time-honored role as a place for personal hygiene. But what really sets kitchens and baths apart from the other rooms is the fact that these are the only rooms that have water moving in and out. In fact water management is the very soul of a kitchen and bath, without which they could not function at all. It comes as no surprise then that understanding the plumbing systems that heat, cool and distribute the water for the various special applications of the kitchen and bath must be a fundamental part of your design skills. The following three chapters give an overview of plumbing systems, from how water gets into and out of the house to the equipment that heats, cools or purifies it to the fixtures that dispense it for household uses.

CHAPTER 6: Hot and Cold Water Supply

Clients don't think about the systems that deliver water to the faucet unless the water smells, leaks, or isn't hot or cold enough. But you must know your way around all those items hidden in walls and floors to make sure your clients get just the right amount of clean water at just the right temperature.

Household plumbing didn't change much until plastic piping and other innovations made it both more economical and easier to install than the older systems based on galvanized steel and cast iron. But the availability of these materials doesn't automatically mean they are acceptable. So one of the first things to do when getting established in your locality is to find out from the local building authority which plumbing codes are in force, then become familiar with the materials they accept.

THE SOURCES OF HOUSEHOLD WATER

Figure 6.1 The water meter and main shutoff valve are usually located in the front yard near the property line.

Water From the Main

Most homes get their water from a municipal supply system managed by a public utility that moves water from reservoirs or storage tanks through a network of piping buried below the streets. Water from the street main to the house flows through a meter and shutoff valve that measures consumption in gallons, then into the house. Utility-supplied water enters the house under pressure of 50 – 60 pounds per square inch (psi) [351 – 421 g/cm²]. For proper function of the fixtures, the pressure should not drop below 30psi (210 g/cm²) or exceed 80psi (g/cm²). The number of fixtures served and how often they are in use at the same time affect the line pressure, as do the length of the piping runs and the number of turns in the system.

Well Water

Rural homes don't have it quite so easy. They must supply their own water from a well that faucets into an underground aquifer. The level of the water varies depending on how much rain has fallen to recharge the aquifer. The level may also drop if other wells near it are withdrawing too much water. During prolonged droughts, the well level may drop below the level of the pump intake. The pump has access to air, not water, and then "goes dry."

Well water quality varies from place to place and from time to time. Whereas utility-supplied water is chlorinated and constantly monitored for quality, well water must be regularly tested by the homeowner for such health hazards as bacteria, nitrates, arsenic, volatile organic compounds (VOCs) and lead.

Various pump designs are available, depending on the depth of the well. Pumps for shallow wells (no deeper than 20 feet (6,096 mm) can sit down into the well itself or inside the basement. Deep (drilled) wells contain the pump at the bottom of the well. In either case, the pump should supply a minimum of 5 gallons (19 L) per minute to ensure an adequate flow rate for the fixtures.

Water from the pump flows into a holding tank equipped with an air bladder. Water pumped into the tank builds up pressure in the air bladder that forces water to the point of use. Without the bladder, the pump would have to cycle on every time a faucet was turned on or the toilet flushed. The tank can be adjusted to yield the same pressure range as that supplied by a public utility.

Figure 6.2 Rural houses often depend on wells for their water. Dug wells are feasible where the water table is consistently within 15 – 30 feet of the surface. Drilled wells are necessary when reliable water is deeper down, often hundreds of feet.

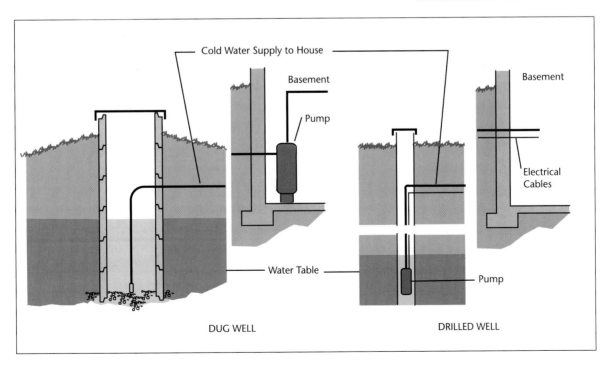

FROM METER TO FAUCET

Traditional Distribution Systems

Cold water enters the house through a supply line at least three quarters of an inch in diameter, or better, a 1-inch diameter pipe. If there is a device to treat the water, it is installed on the main supply line near the point of entry, except for water softeners. This is because the minerals that make water difficult for washing purposes also make it taste good. So water softeners are usually installed on the line that supplies the water heater. The cold water line remains un-softened for drinking. After leaving the water heater, the hot and cold water pipes run parallel to the various take-off points where smaller-diameter branch pipes, or risers, feed individual fixtures and appliances. The rule of thumb for sizing branch piping is 1/2-inch diameter for one or two fixtures/appliances and 3/4-inch diameter for three fixtures/appliances. If your tub, spa or whirlpool requires a 3/4-inch filler, make sure the branch feeder equals this diameter.

Hot and cold supply lines usually run horizontally under framed floors, with supply branches, or **risers**, running up through walls to feed the fixtures.

Water supply piping in houses with slab-on-grade construction may be located below the slab, if PEX plastic piping is used, stubbing up through the walls to feed fixtures, or located in the ceiling and stubbed down (this method allows access for repairs and alterations). However any piping in a ceiling should be tucked under the attic insulation, to protect it from freezing (hot water piping is more efficient, regardless of location, if it is encased in foam insulation). Another goal of pipe layout is to minimize the length of pipe runs and number of fittings the water must course through on its way to the point of use. This ensures minimal friction in the line for maximum pressure at the point of use. To achieve this goal, rooms with water-using fixtures should be close to each other. Fixtures in these rooms should back up to common walls. For example, if a laundry can go near a kitchen, try to locate the kitchen sink on the common wall, with the washer backing up to it.

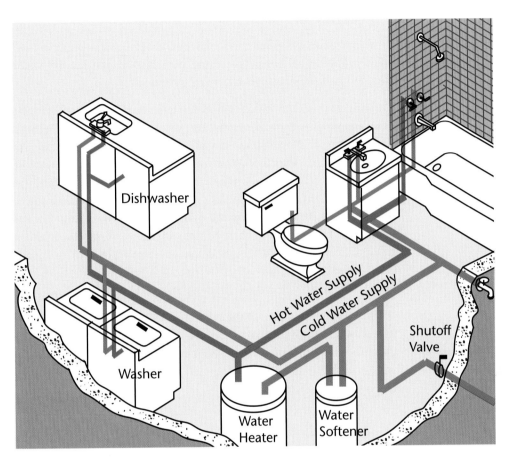

Dishwasher

Hot Water Supply

Cold Water Supply

Shutoff
Valve

Washer

Water
Heater

Water
Softener

Fixtures inevitably need maintenance, repair or replacement at some time or another. When that time comes, the water supply to the fixture must be shut off, even for minor repairs such as replacing a washer in a faucet. A shut-off valve installed on the hot and cold supply pipe just before the fixture enables work on the fixture to occur without shutting down the entire water supply system.

Figure 6.3 In a traditional water-piping system, branch pipes tap off the central supply pipe to bring hot and cold water to each fixture.

Manifold Distribution Systems

Traditional galvanized steel or copper distribution piping—parallel hot and cold supply lines with branches to each fixture—requires many fittings for changes in direction and intersections with branch piping. With all fixtures installed off the main supply pipes, the line pressure can drop when several fixtures are used simultaneously.

A newer method for residential water distribution overcomes this drawback. Instead of a central line with tap-off points, the system starts with a distribution manifold that distributes water through separate lines to each fixture, so that the path from each fixture to the source is a "home run." Manifold piping systems are made possible by flexible plastic piping that can snake around bends without elbows and other fittings. The flexibility of the pipe also eliminates the water hammer associated with metal piping systems.

There are two manifolds. The cold-water manifold connects to the main supply pipe from the meter. The hot-water manifold connects to the water heater. Branch lines faucet off the manifolds and run directly to each fixture. Manifolds are 1-inch diameter (larger than most service lines) to ensure adequate water flow to the fixtures. Because these systems make a direct run to each fixture, they require fewer fittings and can thus use smaller diameter supply piping for the home runs, typically 3/8 inch. A continuous, built-in reservoir provides equalized water flow and helps maintain constant pressure to the supply lines. If there is not a shutoff valve for each home run at the manifold, one should be provided at the fixture, as in a traditional system.

Figure 6.4 Manifold water distribution systems make a direct home run of hot and cold water lines to each fixture from a central distribution manifold. Flexible plastic piping makes pipe runs of this sort feasible.

Some manifolds also feature fixture shut-off valves allowing the user to shut off the water to individual fixtures from one location. Others—semi-home run or termination manifolds—are less complicated and may suffice for a few rooms and reduce the number of fittings required in the plumbing system.

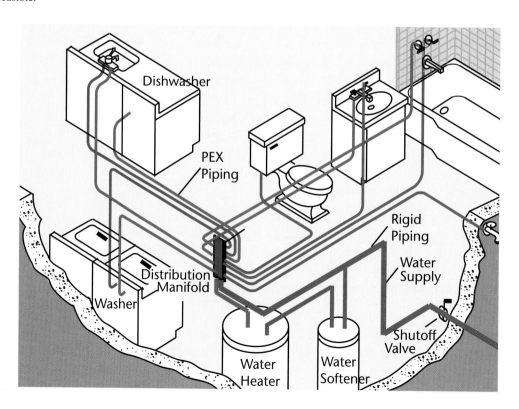

PIPING FOR WATER SUPPLY

Quality piping will withstand temperature extremes, corrosion and the buildup of minerals (scale) that eventually constrict the flow of water. Your plumbing code spells out what's acceptable for a particular application. Here's a brief run-down of residential water-supply pipe materials, from the tried-and-true to the emerging technologies.

Lead

Common for water-supply piping in the 1900s, lead was gradually replaced by galvanized steel. It turns up today only in some lead mains and service piping of old inner city neighborhoods. Because of the known health hazards of lead it is now illegal for water-supply piping as well as most other construction products.

Galvanized Steel

Galvanized steel piping is mild steel coated with zinc to resist corrosion. It comes in straight lengths that are joined by threaded connectors, or fittings. Numerous types of fittings—elbows, tees, wyes and reducers—suit the size of pipe and requirements of the joint.

Installing steel pipe is difficult and expensive—the main reason it has been supplanted by copper and other materials. Other flaws include vulnerability to oxidation, or rust, both inside and out. Oxidation reduces the interior diameter of the pipe, which then restricts the flow of water. In turn, joints weaken, and may leak. Galvanized steel piping fails sooner at the heavier-used fixtures of the kitchen and bath. The more a fixture is used, the more water and oxygen are present to oxidize, or corrode, the piping. Failure shows up first as round-shaped rust growths ("rust warts") on the outside of the pipe. These are failures that have come through the pipe. It is not unusual for the corrosion to seal the failure. If you encounter a home with a steel pipe water system that is failing, you can specify copper for the portions to be remodeled, but the best approach is to replace the whole system if feasible.

Copper

Copper reigns as the most common water-supply piping in houses today. Copper piping comes in rigid, straight lengths and as flexible tubing. Copper or brass fittings are used for both types, but flexible tubing uses fewer fittings, since it bends to change direction. In fact, care must be taken not to kink the soft metal. There are two types of fittings. One type slips over the end of the pipe and bonds to the pipe when solder is applied with a flame. Another type uses compression

71

gaskets plus a threaded nut. This type is used to join pipes of a dissimilar metal or at a joint that must be disconnected from time to time, such as the connection to a flexible stainless steel pipe from a sink or toilet.

Copper is a very dependable material. But acidic water—water with a low pH level—corrodes the metal. When the walls of the pipe wear thin, the failures will look like tiny, round, green patina stains. If these stains are ignored, water may spray through the hole in the center of the round stain. This problem is generally due to acidic water, which should be neutralized by a water softener.

There are three types of copper piping for domestic water supply, which vary by the thickness of the walls. The thickest, **Type K**, is identified by a green stripe, is for in-ground water supply piping. Blue-banded **Type L** (medium thick) and red-banded **Type M** (the thinnest) are used for indoor water supply Check with your code authority for specific requirements in your area.

Threaded Brass

Piping made from threaded brass is uncommon, but occasionally shows up in homes built before 1940. However threaded brass is widely used for fittings for copper pipe. The same agents that deteriorate copper tend to do the same to brass.

Polybutylene (PB)

Plastic piping has made steady inroads into home water-supply systems in recent years, because of its greater economy over steel and copper. But not all types work equally well. Polybutylene (PB) piping is a flexible gray or black piping made from polybutylene plastic. Joints fit together with either epoxy or insert fittings and metal crimp rings. Barbed brass or copper insert fittings with crimp ring joints are generally more dependable than the epoxy joints. The joints are vulnerable to chlorine in the water, which causes the plastic to deteriorate. Since its debut in home plumbing systems in the 1970s, subsequent failures of the product have resulted in several individual and class action lawsuits in the U.S. Most municipalities do not currently allow certain types of PB piping for residential potable water.

Polyethylene (PE)

Polyethylene (PE) piping is approved only for cold water systems. Typical uses include service piping from a municipal main or household well. Generally black in color, PE piping is a flexible material easier to install than most other service-piping materials. PE pipe sections join together by two stainless steel band clamps. Originally made for radiant floor heating systems in the 1970s, PE pipe began to rupture under exposure to chlorine, causing costly demolition of the concrete slabs that overlaid the piping.

Cross-Linked Polyethylene (PEX)

An improved version of PE piping was achieved in the 1980s by a process in which the molecules in the plastic were cross linked to form a more durable material. Cross-linked polyethylene (PEX) piping is typically joined by crimp fittings, but compression fittings are also used. After 20 years of accelerated testing, PEX has yet to fail under normal conditions. It is the current favorite material for sub-slab radiant floor heating systems and is fast becoming popular for domestic hot and cold water supply. PEX is now accepted for potable water use by codes in most areas. Though the pipe itself costs as much as copper, it installs more quickly for big savings in labor. Its flexibility makes PEX a good candidate for the manifold distribution layouts mentioned earlier.

Polyvinyl Chloride (PVC)

Polyvinyl Chloride (PVC) piping is a white semi-rigid plastic joined by fittings bonded with a primer and PVC solvent. PVC is approved for cold water only, which explains why it is popular for irrigation systems outside the house. Another version called chlorinated polyvinyl chloride (CPVC) is acceptable for both cold and hot water, as long as the temperature stays under 140°F (60°C).

COMPARING WATER
SUPPLY PIPE MATERIALS

COMPARING WATER SUPPLY PIPE MATERIALS				
Material	Uses	Connections	Pros	Cons
Lead	(no longer legal)			Toxic
Galvanized Steel	Water service, hot and cold water	Threaded galvanized steel fittings	Strong	High cost. Corroded by acidic water, hard water causes scale, water hammer
Copper	Water service, hot and cold water	Soldered or compression fittings of copper or brass	Fast, easy to assemble (especially tubing), corrosion resistant	Not very good with very hard or very soft water, joints can be damaged by water hammer
Threaded Brass	Hot and cold water	Threaded brass	Corrosion resistant	High cost
Polybutylene (PB)	Hot and cold water	Epoxy, inserts + crimp rings	Few fittings, no freeze damage, no water hammer	Must keep away from heat ducts and flues, joints prone to failure
Cross-Linked Polyethylene (PEX)	Water service, hot and cold water	Inserts + crimp rings	Same pros as PB, but improved, longer lasting	
Polyvinyl Chloride (PVC)	Cold water	PVC fittings joined with solvent cement	Low cost, lightweight	Cold water only, requires protection from heat sources
Chlorinated Polyvinyl Chloride (CPVC)	Hot and cold water	CPVC fittings joined with solvent cement	Same as PVC plus can use for hot water	Protect from heat
Polyethylene (PE)	Cold water	Stainless steel clamps	Low cost, lightweight, good from well to house	Cold water only

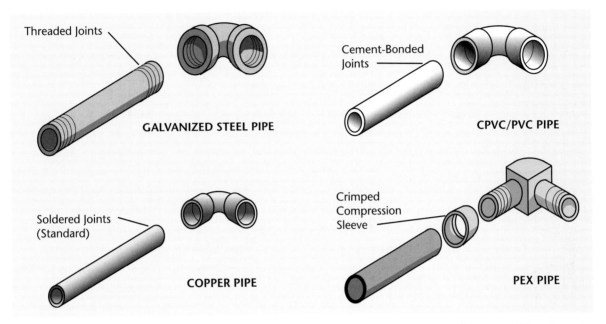

Threaded Joints

GALVANIZED STEEL PIPE

Cement-Bonded Joints

CPVC/PVC PIPE

Soldered Joints (Standard)

COPPER PIPE

Crimped Compression Sleeve

PEX PIPE

Figure 6.5 Four materials make up the bulk of most residential water systems. Copper still reigns as the most popular for new construction, while PEX is gaining due to its flexibility and ease of installation.

SIZING PIPE FOR WATER SUPPLY

Sizing Pipe for Water Supply	
House Main	1"
House Service	3/4"
Supply Riser	3/4"
Kitchen Sink	1/2"
Ice Maker	1/4"
Dishwasher	3/8"
Clothes Washer	1/2"
Shower	1/2"
Tub, spa, whirlpool	1/2", 3/4"
Toilet	3/8", 1/2"
Lavatory	3/8", 1/2"

WATER SUPPLY PROBLEMS AND SOLUTIONS

It takes more than the right pipe and fittings to make a good water-supply system. Several things can cause a water-supply system to malfunction or deteriorate. Here are two of which you should be aware of.

Water Hammer

Water is not much of an elastic material. While it expands and contracts some when heated or cooled, it doesn't have the same amount of "give" as air. A sudden shutoff of the water supply to an appliance or fixture can abruptly halt the flow of water in the pipes. The resulting jolt, or "water hammer," causes an annoying noise. In time, repeated water hammer shocks can loosen joints that result in leaks.

Water hammer is easy to prevent. The key is to build in something in the piping that can absorb the sudden shock of the water's momentum. There are two ways to do this. One is a loop or coil of the piping itself, which acts like a spring to absorb the shock of the water hammer. The other is a special device that contains an air chamber. Installed in the supply piping to a fixture, the air compresses to cushion shocks to the system.

Figure 6.6 Two remedies for water hammer. The expansion device (left) allows the pipe itself to expand and contract to absorb the sudden differences in water pressure. The air chamber (right) absorbs the shock because the air in the chamber expands and contracts.

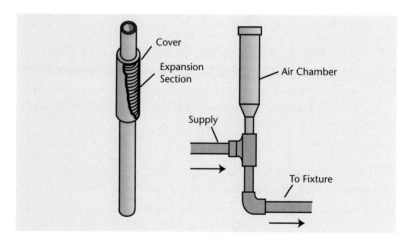

Dissimilar Pipe Connections

Remodeling work often entails joining existing piping of one material to new piping of another. This is possible, but only with the right kind of fitting. Dissimilar metals can corrode when they are in contact with each other. The small amount of acid in the water sets up an electrolytic action between the two metals, causing electrons from one to flow to the other. A copper-to-steel joint is a likely point of failure. The solution is to keep the two metals apart. A **dielectric union** separates the two by placing a plastic collar and rubber washer —both non-metals—between them.

After you have done everything right to get the water to the fixtures and appliances efficiently, you'll want to make sure the water itself is safe to drink and suitable for other uses, such as cleansing.

Numerous contaminants can impede reaching this goal. The problem is most serious in well water. Water from a public utility is treated against biological organisms. But even centrally treated water can be unsafe. In 1993, 400,000 people in Milwaukee became ill from cryptosporidium ingestion and 104 died. The system was contaminated by runoff from heavy storms that overwhelmed the filtration plant. Reports of less extreme events of this sort crop up more and more these days. On the whole, North Americans probably have the cleanest drinking water in the world. Yet problems do occur and our growing population and encroachment into watershed areas can only make matters worse.

Households can respond by either having their drinking water delivered by a bottled water service or by installing a point-of-use (POU) treatment device to counter contaminants that may be unhealthy or simply objectionable.

The Pollutants

The Safe Drinking Water Act passed by the U.S. Congress in 1974 spelled out maximum safe levels for 22 known contaminants. Yet, more than 200 substances have been found in drinking water. The risks these pose to human health are known and well documented for some contaminants, such as the following:

Lead at even low levels is a hazard to health, particularly in children. A cumulative poison, lead can damage the nervous system, internal organs and cause anemia. Drinking water is one of the ways we ingest lead. Lead probably gets into most houses today from lead-based solder used in copper water pipes (codes now require lead-free solder). A less likely source might be the pipe from the main in the street to the house or—in very old houses—lead water pipes. Soft (acidic) water dissolves more lead out of these conduits than hard water.

Arsenic may enter the home from well water that has flowed through arsenic-rich rocks. Industrial effluents also contribute arsenic to water in some places. Inorganic arsenic is mostly found as trivalent arsenite. Organic arsenic species, abundant in seafood, are very much less harmful to health and are readily eliminated by the body. Chronic arsenic poisoning from long-term exposure through drinking water causes cancer of the skin, lungs, urinary bladder and kidney, as well as other skin changes such as pigmentation changes and thickening. Increased risks of lung and bladder cancer and of arsenic-associated skin lesions have been observed at drinking water arsenic concentrations of less than 0.05 mg/L.

Trihalomethanes (THM) comprise a group of chemicals that cause cancer in laboratory animals. This group includes **chlorine** when found in excessive amounts. Chlorine has proven an effective purification agent in public water supplies since 1908. While the amount added to treat water is probably too low to pose a risk to health, some studies have suggested it might be a contributing factor to bladder cancer. Whether or not there is any substance to this, we do know that chlorine makes water taste bad. The EPA now restricts the total maximum concentrations of THM to 0.1 mg/L.

Nitrates are by-products of fertilizer that can leach into ground water and contaminate the aquifers that supply both public and private-source drinking water. High nitrate levels in drinking water can pose a special risk for infants. When an infant takes in nitrate, it's converted into another compound called nitrite. Nitrite reduces the blood's ability to carry oxygen. The result is a condition known as methemoglobinemia, or "blue baby syndrome." Public water is tested and treated for nitrates, but private well water is vulnerable, particularly if the well is located in an agricultural area.

Pesticides are another concern in rural areas and a special danger for private wells. Pesticides not taken up by plants, adsorbed by soils or broken down by sunlight, soil organisms or chemical reactions may ultimately get into the ground water. Contamination can result from using high concentrations of water-soluble pesticides for a specific crop in a vulnerable area. The hazard to human health depends upon the kind and amount of pesticide, how long a person has been consuming the water and the person's overall health. Acute pesticide poisoning symptoms may include headaches, dizziness, stomach and intestinal upset, numbness of extremities, spasms, convulsions and heart attacks. While the long-term, chronic effects of pesticides in humans are not completely understood, some pesticides are suspected of causing cancer.

Other contaminants may pose health hazards from minor to severe or simply make the water taste or smell bad. You should probably recommend that your clients have their water tested before you complete the design, so that you can help them select the appropriate point-of-use (POU) treatment device. There are many sources of information on water quality and testing facilities. For local help, check with the Cooperative Extension Service in your local or state government. The EPA is a repository for a vast wealth of information on a number of issues relating to water quality. You can phone their water quality hotline at 800-426-4791 or contact them at their Internet address, hotline-sdwa@epa.gov.

Treatment Options

The report from a testing service will spell out the levels of various contaminants in the water and thereby suggest the most effective treatment. POU devices treat water by one or more of five basic techniques. While each has its pros and cons, there, unfortunately is no silver bullet that zaps all contaminants.

Mechanical filtration devices remove dirt, sediment and loose scale from the incoming water by straining it through a sieve made of ceramic material, sand, filter paper, or compressed glass wool. The result is better looking, better tasting, better smelling water, but not necessarily healthier water.

Activated carbon filtration removes organic compounds such as chloroform, pesticides, benzene and trichloroethylene. Activated carbon filters also take out chlorine and improve the water's taste and color. They do not eliminate bacteria. The filters consist of carbon granules with many exposed pores that trap certain contaminants. With use, some pores clog and decrease the filter's efficiency. Filter cartridges must eventually be replaced. However, their length of service time depends on the design, volume of water processed and length of time in use.

Reverse osmosis purifies water by passing it through a semi-permeable membrane under normal faucet pressure. Up to 95% of dissolved contaminants are eliminated. Some membranes even reject many types of bacteria. Reverse osmosis under-sink devices are costly both to install and to operate. They contain three cartridges—one for particulates, one for activated carbon and the reverse osmosis membrane—each with a different useful life, so replacement is a chore.

Less expensive countertop models contain a three-in-one cartridge. These units connect to the faucet via a diverter valve. Though effective, reverse osmosis filtration is slow and wasteful. Six hours produce a single gallon of water, while four to six gallons of wastewater go down the drain. Countertop models yield about three quarts (2.8 L) in just over four hours. Because they use normal pressure in the water line to operate, they need no outside energy.

Distillation heats water to steam, then condenses it back to liquid form, purging most of the contaminants in the process. This is the only purification method that removes microorganisms and trace amounts of heavy metals with absolute certainty. Even so, certain volatile organic chemicals that have a lower boiling point than water—such as some pesticides—vaporize with the water, re-condense and end up in the processed water anyway. Because distilled water contains no minerals, its taste suffers. It is also very soft and aggressive towards metals in pipes. Distillers are powered by electricity and have a stainless steel, glass or plastic reservoir with capacities ranging from 1.5 to 15 gallons (5.7 L – 56.8 L). Slow and costly to operate, they are also vulnerable to mineral build-up from hard water.

Ion Exchange is used to soften hard water. Hard water gets its name because it's hard to make lather with soap. The hardness comes from the mineral salts it contains, mainly calcium and magnesium. These minerals react with soap to form greasy rings in bathtubs and washbasins. When heated, the minerals turn to hard scale that builds up on pots and pans and the insides of pipes, hot water tanks and boilers. We measure water hardness in grains per gallon (gpg) or milligrams per liter (mg/L). Multiply gpg x 17.1 to get mg/L. Moderately hard water contains 3.6 – 7.0 gpg (61 – 120 mg/L). Very hard water contains 7.0 – 10.5 gpg (121 – 180 mg/L).

While detergents cut through hard water, a water softener can wipe out the problem entirely and should be considered if water hardness exceeds 10.5 gpg (180 mg/L). However, water softened too much—to zero hardness—is corrosive.

Water softeners work by a process called ion exchange, where the hard water passes through a bed of softening material charged with sodium ions. The hardening minerals are attracted to the softening material and held there. At the same time, sodium releases into the water (a possible hazard to people who must restrict their intake of sodium or salt). In time, the operation of the softener depletes the sodium and it must be recharged. Salt brine flushed through the bed drives out the hardness and replaces it with sodium. Rinsed with fresh water, the renewed ion exchange material is once again ready for action.

Most water softeners use a timer to start the regenerating process automatically. The homeowner need only add salt to the brine tank periodically to ensure a constant supply of softened water. Devices come in various capacities, according to the size of the family and projected water usage.

COMPARING WATER TREATMENT OPTIONS   Data from EPA

Contaminant	Maximum Contaminant Level	Mechanical Filtration	Activated Carbon Filters	Reverse Osmosis	Distillation	Ion Exchange (Water Softener)
Arsenic	0.05 mg/L			•	•	
Asbestos	7 mg			•	•	
Atrazine	0.003 mg/L		•	•		
Benzene	0.005 mg/L		•			
Fluoride	4 mg/L			•	•	
Lead	0.015 mg/L*			•	•	•
Mercury	0.002 mg/L		•	•	•	
Nitrates	10 mg/L			•	•	
Radium	5 pC/L			•	•	•
Radon	300 pC/L		•			
Trichloroethylene	0.005 mg/L		•		•	
Total Trihalomethanes	0.1 mg/L		•		•	
Bacteria and viruses			•	•	•	
Cryptosporidium/giardia				•	•	
Metallic taste				•	•	•
Objectionable taste				•	•	
Objectionable odor			•			
Color		•	•	•	•	•
Sediment	0.5 – 1.0 NTU**	•				

*EPA action level   **Performance standard

81

WATER HEATING

Clients today demand a reliable supply of hot water for showers, bathtubs, dishwashers and laundry equipment, and there are a variety of systems to supply it. There are water heaters that are independent of other equipment and water heaters integrated with other equipment. There is also variety when it comes to energy source, though electricity and gas fuel most residential water heating in the U.S. and Canada.

Tank-Type Water Heaters

Conventional water heaters with their own tanks are the workhorses for most homes. Basically simple devices, they consist of a thermostatically controlled burner (gas units) or heating element (electric units) that heats the water. An insulated tank stores a ready supply of hot water. Tanks are typically lined with glass to prevent the hot water from corroding the metal. Tank capacities range from 30 to 82 gallons (114 L – 311 L). Because the supply has to serve the maximum usage, the right size water heater for a family depends on peak usage, which usually occurs in the early morning or evening. You can get a fair idea of an adequate capacity in gallons (or liters) from the table, "Estimating Water Heater Capacity," adapted from guidelines of the Gas Appliance Manufacturers Association.

ESTIMATING WATER HEATER CAPACITY					
Use	Required gallons (liters)	x	Number of users per hour	=	Gallons (liters) used in one hour
Shower	20 gal. (76 L)	x		=	
Bath	20 gal. (76 L)	x		=	
Shaving	2 (8 L)	x		=	
Hands/Face Washing	4 (15 L)	x		=	
Hair Shampoo	4 (15 L)	x		=	
Automatic Dishwasher	14 (53 L)	x		=	
	Total peak hour demand				

To illustrate, let's plug in some values for a household of two adults and one child for the time in the morning when they are getting ready for the day's activities:

2 persons showering	20 gal. x 2 = 40 gal.
1 person shaving	2 gal. x 1 = 2 gal.
1 person shampooing	4 gal. x 1 = 4 gal.
1 person washing hands/face	4 gal. x 1 = 4 gal.
	Total peak hour demand: 50 gal.

A 50-gallon tank should work for this family. If the family had a couple of teenagers, the use would naturally go up. In addition to the tank volume, tank-type water heaters also vary in their recovery rate, the amount of water in gallons per hour raised at a given efficiency and Btu input. Manufacturers' specifications state this data for each model. It's better to choose a size a few gallons greater than the estimate to ensure the clients have enough hot water at peak times. But an excessively large tank size just wastes money on fuel. The selected model should operate at a maximum pressure of 160 psi (1103 kPa) and heat water to a maximum 210°F (99°C), over the 115°F (46°C) temperature considered the safe maximum for use at the faucet. The only appliance in the house that requires higher temperatures is the dishwasher, which has its own water heater. Most water heaters are shipped at a factory-preset temperature of 120°F (49°C) with a provision for higher adjustment if the homeowner desires.

A burner in a combustion chamber below the tank heats the water in a gas water heater. The combustion gasses rise up through a flue in the tank and through another flue that exits through the walls or roof. Electric water heaters contain one or two heating elements called electrodes that project through the wall of the tank into the water. The higher the wattage and voltage of the element, the faster the water will heat. Heated by electricity resistance, the elements produce no exhaust gasses, so need no flue. This feature makes them ideal for locating centrally to the rooms that use hot water—the bath, laundry and kitchen. They can safely sit inside a closet, for example, where code would not permit a gas heater. Alas, these rooms are seldom close to each other, so some designers prefer to locate the main water heater close to the bath and have a second water heater close to or in the kitchen, either in a crawl space or under the kitchen sink. The second unit can be a 20-gallon tank-type water heater or a tankless one, as discussed further on.

Figure 6.7 A gas tank-type water heater requires a gas supply and a flue that conducts exhaust to the exterior.

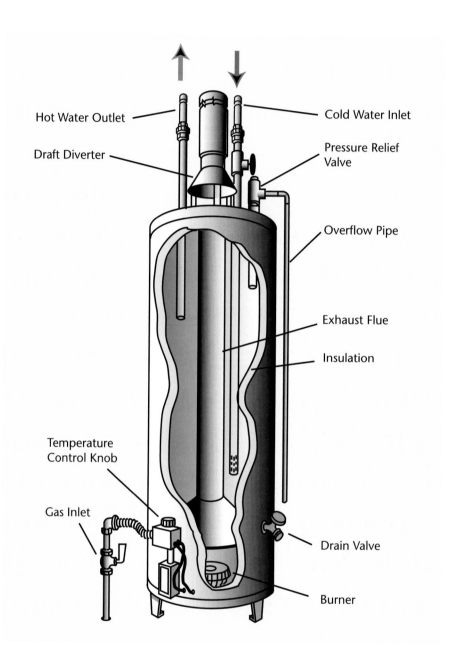

Hot Water Outlet
Draft Diverter
Cold Water Inlet
Pressure Relief Valve
Overflow Pipe
Exhaust Flue
Insulation
Temperature Control Knob
Gas Inlet
Drain Valve
Burner

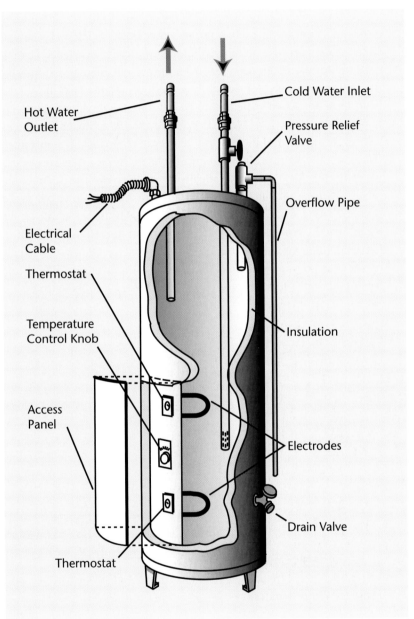

Figure 6.8 An electric tank-type water heater.

Hot Water Outlet

Cold Water Inlet

Pressure Relief Valve

Electrical Cable

Overflow Pipe

Thermostat

Temperature Control Knob

Insulation

Access Panel

Electrodes

Thermostat

Drain Valve

The same technology that powers refrigeration and air conditioning also works to heat water. **Heat pump water heaters (HPWHs)**, unlike water heaters that use either gas burners or electric resistance heating coils to heat the water, take heat from the surrounding air and transfer it to the water in the tank. Much less energy is required to "move" the heat than to actually heat the water unless the surrounding air temperature is very low. Most HPWHs have back-up heating elements to heat the water during very low temperature periods. Because they consume only half to a third as much electricity as a typical electric water heater, they save dramatically on fuel costs. The savings are offset, however, by much higher initial costs. Another downside is the rate of heating. HPWHs heat water more slowly than electric or gas water heaters, typically about 15 gallons per hour. HPWHs install in two configurations. Both extract heat from room air. One system expels the now-cooled air back into the room—a disadvantage during the heating season. The other type expels the cooled air to the outside.

Figure 6.9 Heat pump water heaters supply hot water efficiently with electricity, typically providing the same amount of hot water at one-half to one-third the energy used by an electric water heater with resistance coils.

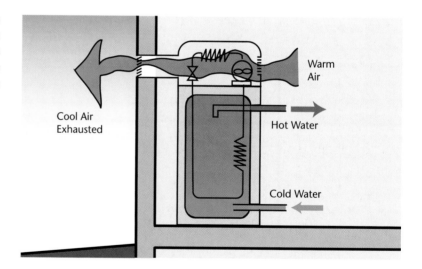

Warm Air

Cool Air Exhausted

Hot Water

Cold Water

Tankless Water Heaters

The cost of heating and storing 50 gallons of water or more in a tank-type water heater is high. An electric water heater in a typical home is the single largest user of electricity. About one fourth of the energy consumed is lost through the tank. More heat gets wasted in long runs of piping between the water heater and fixtures, particularly if they are distant from the unit. Remote fixtures may wait up to 45 seconds before hot water emerges, while the "warm-up" water gets wasted down the drain. These flaws make a **tankless** (also called **point-of-use, instantaneous, on-demand**) water heater worth considering in some cases. Available in both gas and electric models, they heat water only when it is called for. Tankless units can be installed centrally or at the point of use, such as under a sink. They never run out of hot water, as can tank-type units, but deliver hot water at a lower flow rate. Even the largest models with capacities of 100,000 – 125,000 Btu can't provide more than 4 gallons per minute (gpm, 15 L/min.) of 100°F (38°C) water or 2 – 3 gpm (7.6 – 11.4 L/min.) of 120°F (49°C) water. These flow rates won't satisfy typical North American hot water habits. Most homeowners are used to using more than one hot-water appliance at a time. Showers draw 2.5 gpm (9.5 L/m) of water at 120°F (49°C), washing dishes demands another 2.5 gpm. A tank water heater can easily accommodate both activities, but a tankless model can't meet the demands of both fixtures simultaneously.

A tankless water heater can, however, make sense as an auxiliary water heater for fixtures distant from the central water heater. Gas units require a 4-, 5-, or 6-inch (102, 127, 152 mm)-diameter flue, rather than the standard 3 inch (76 mm) vent of a tank-type heater. They draw large amounts of combustion air, which makes under-sink or closet installations dubious. Consult the manufacturer's specifications for make-up air and piping requirements.

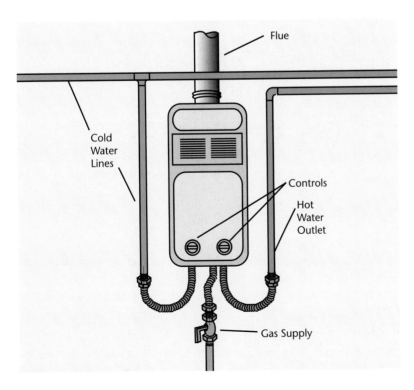

Figure 6.10 Tankless (demand, or instantaneous) water heaters heat water only when it is being used, thus saving the energy lost through distribution piping and saving up to 20% of the fuel required for tank-type water heaters. They make the best sense for fixtures located far from the home's central water heater, or as substitutes for a central heater.

Integrated Water Heating

Houses heated by a gas- or oil-fired boiler can do without a separate water heater of any type if the boiler is equipped with a domestic hot water loop inside the boiler. As with a tankless system, hot water is produced at a constant rate and temperature, as it flows through the loop. The downside is that the flow rate is often too slow for more than one fixture operating at any one time. A separate insulated tank added to the system for storage solves the problem, but the hybrid system may then not have much edge over a separate, conventional water heater with its own heat source.

CHAPTER 7: Drain, Waste and Vent Systems

Getting the water to the appliances is one half of a home plumbing system. The other half entails getting it out of the house. This is the function of the drain, waste and vent (DWV) system. Note how this system differs from the piping that supplies water:

1. Waste pipes slope to enable flow by gravity alone, rather than pressure.

2. Piping must be larger to accommodate solids as well as liquids.

3. The DWV system must have means of preventing sewer gas from flowing back into the house.

In this chapter we'll see how each of the components of the DWV system work together to meet these objectives.

PARTS OF THE SYSTEM

The network of piping that carries waste out of the house makes up the **drainage** and **waste** parts of the DWV system. It begins with small-diameter **drain piping** at the fixtures that feed into branch pipes of a larger size, then into a vertical **soil stack**, a pipe usually 4 inches in diameter, which carries the waste down to the **house drain**, a horizontal pipe of the same size as the stack, which leads to the municipal sewer system or septic tank if the home is beyond reach of a municipal sewer network.

A septic tank buried near the house receives the sewage and holds it while bacteria and other organisms partially digest the waste. In the process, the undigested solids drop to the bottom of the tank as sludge, while the liquid effluent runs out the top of the tank to the drain, or leach field. There, a network of piping or shaped conduits receives the liquid effluent and distributes it into the soil, where it further breaks down and purifies.

When adding fixtures to a home with a septic tank, check to make sure the septic tank is big enough for the additional load. A food waste disposer imposes an excessive load on the septic system and many plumbers advise against it. The general consensus is that the system should either be oversized by 50% or cleaned out twice as often as it would have without the disposer.

Waste Piping

We spoke of "vertical" and "horizontal" piping, but the horizontal pipes can't be dead level or they won't drain. Codes require horizontal branches to slope a minimum of 1/4 inch (6 mm) per foot.

The diameters of drainage pipes vary according to where they are in the system. The smallest ones come off the kitchen and bath sinks and are usually 1 1/4-inch or, preferred, 1 1/2-inch diameter. Showers, bathtubs and washing machines typically have drains 1 1/2-inch or 2-inch diameter, while toilet drains are 3 or 4 inches. The stack and main sewer pipe are the largest pipes in the system and usually 4 inches in diameter. Bigger is not always better for drain pipes and can slow the flow of sewage, so find out from the plumbing inspector in your area which pipe sizes are required for various applications.

Pipes in a DWV system are always straight. Changes in direction are made with a fitting of the right shape. Plumbers speak of **els**, L-shaped fittings for making 90° turns; **wyes**, fittings that have two outlets at a 30° or 45° angle; and **tees**, fittings that allow a tap from a branch into a main line.

Codes require cleanouts at the ends of horizontal piping runs where they change direction more than 45°. All cleanouts must have at least 18 inches (457 mm) of clearance to allow access for cleaning rods, snakes and other tools.

Traps

The third charge we gave the DWV system was preventing sewer gas from flowing back into the house. U-shaped traps at each fixture do this by retaining a water seal in the bottom of the "U." The seal not only keeps unpleasant gasses out of the living spaces, but also bars rodents from entering the house via the sewer pipes.

Plumbing codes require every fixture to have a trap. Toilets have a trap built into the structure of the fixture. Traps for other fixtures occur in the drainpipe just below the fixture. The most common type is shaped like the letter "P" lying on its side and is called a **P-trap**. Codes typically require traps to have a water seal of between 2 inches and 4 inches, be self-cleaning and not depend on moving parts. Also, no trap outlet can be larger than the fixture drain it serves. Traps must be level with their water seals. Though each fixture must have its own trap, a single trap can serve some side-by-side fixtures, such as a double sink.

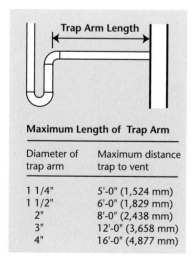

Maximum Length of Trap Arm

Diameter of trap arm	Maximum distance trap to vent
1 1/4"	5'-0" (1,524 mm)
1 1/2"	6'-0" (1,829 mm)
2"	8'-0" (2,438 mm)
3"	12'-0" (3,658 mm)
4"	16'-0" (4,877 mm)

Figure 7.1 Maximum length of trap arm.

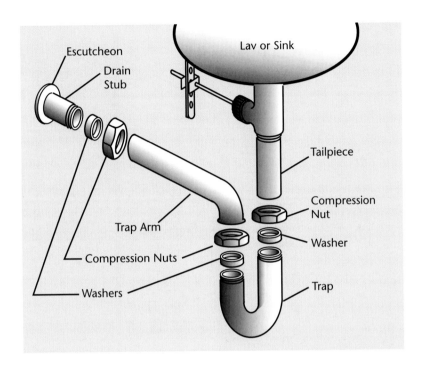

Figure 7.2 Typical drain assembly for a sink or lavatory. P-traps are the currently accepted method of providing a water seal.

Vents

Traps only work if they stay full. But if they were simply connected to the piping downstream in a completely sealed environment, the water flowing down would suck out the water in the trap, leaving if filled with air. To prevent the trap from being siphoned in this manner, we vent the system beyond the trap to equalize the pressure. The vent also allows sewer gas to escape to the outdoors.

Codes require the drains of each fixture to be vented and also specify the minimum size of the vent pipe. The minimum size of any vent can never be smaller than 1 inch or the diameter of the drain it serves, whichever is larger. Beyond that, the kind of fixture, diameter of the drain being vented and length of vent pipe all factor in to the required size. Houses typically have a 3- or 4-inch main soil stack that extends up to vent through the roof.

Figure 7.3 A typical DWV system for a multi-story house.

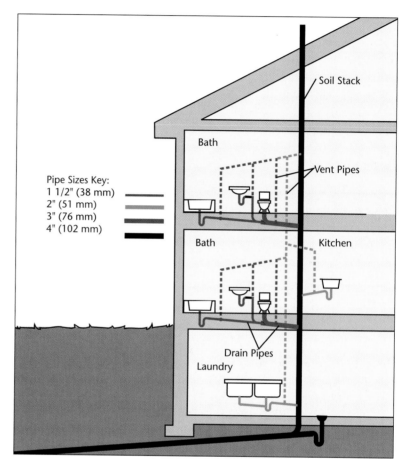

Figure 7.4 The maximum distance between a trap and the vent pipe depends on the diameter of the trap arm piping.

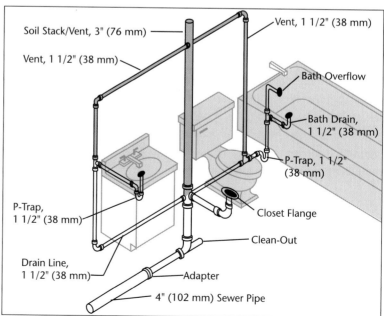

HOW DO YOU VENT AN ISLAND SINK?

Vent piping normally installs in walls behind fixtures. This works fine for fixtures that back up to a wall, but not for sinks in islands or peninsulas. If a fixture is further than a code-specified maximum distance from a vent pipe in a wall—typically 8 feet (2,438 mm) for a 2-inch diameter drain—it must contain its own vent. Here are three ways to do that. (Always check with your local plumbing inspector for what is allowed in your area).

Single-Fixture Wet Vent

In a wet vent, the P-trap from the sink runs horizontally into a larger vertical pipe in the sink base cabinet and discharges into a 3- or 4-inch drain line located in the floor. The drain line must have a cleanout upstream from the entry tee. This system works because oversizing the drain lines beyond the P-trap increases the free-air capacity of the drain, allowing the sink to drain without siphoning out the water in the trap.

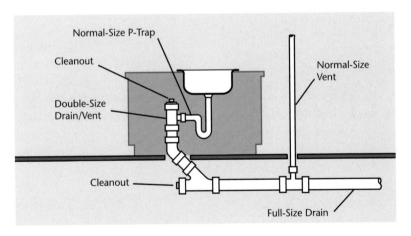

Normal-Size P-Trap

Cleanout

Double-Size
Drain/Vent

Normal-Size
Vent

Cleanout

Full-Size Drain

Figure 7.5 An island sink can be wet-vented if the trap runs into a vertical pipe at least twice the diameter of the trap before connecting with the main drain and vent piping.

Bow Vent

Another approach is to connect the P-trap outlet to a vent, as if it backed up to a wall. But instead of the vent continuing up through the countertop, the portion above the trap loops back down to connect with a remote vent that *is* in a wall. The portion of the vent below the P-trap connects to a drain pipe below the floor. The main drawback of this arrangement is the large amount of space inside the cabinet consumed by the bow vent.

Figure 7.6 A bow vent near the sink is another way to vent an island sink but uses a lot of space in the cabinet.

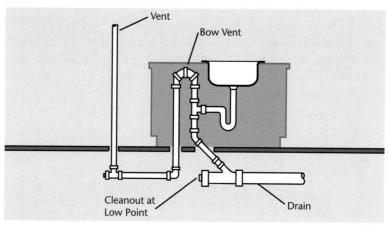

Automatic Vent

The simplest way out of the dilemma is a device that works as a one-way check valve to let make-up air into the system as the sink drains. Automatic, or "bladder" vents are typically glued to the end of the short vertical vent pipe that rises above the P-trap. But if the mechanical valve fails, it will permeate the room with sewer gas.

Figure 7.7 The simplest and most space-saving way to vent an island sink is with an automatic one-way check valve that admits make-up air into the system. Always check with your plumbing inspector to find out which devices are acceptable.

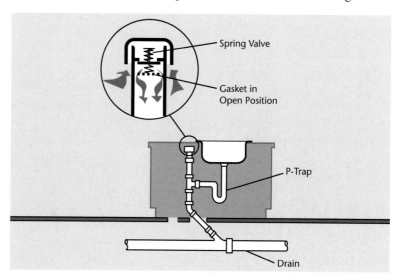

DWV PIPE MATERIALS

Just as plastics are replacing metals in water supply piping, they have mostly edged out traditional cast iron waste piping in homes because of their greater economy and ease of installation. However, while plastic pipe is cheaper and easier to install than metal, it is not necessarily a better material, as we'll see below.

Cast Iron, the Old Faithful

Cast iron has been used for indoor waste piping ever since houses had indoor plumbing. In early installations, pipe sections had one straight end and the other end flared into a hub shape. The straight (spigot) end of the previous pipe fitted into the hub of the next pipe. The joint was sealed by first tamping a bituminous-impregnated hemp rope called oakum into it, then pouring molten lead into the joint. The lead and oakum joint is rare today, replaced by joints that rely on compression gaskets to make the seal. Compression gaskets also enable a cast iron pipe to be joined to pipe of other materials—a plus in old houses undergoing alteration.

Cast iron pipe is strong, durable, and heat-resistant to the point of being fireproof. Used for the main waste-vent stack in a house, it is much quieter than plastic. This can be important in some installations, such as if the main stack is located in a wall near the living room. The sound of a sudden burst of water plunging down the pipe every time a toilet is flushed upstairs comes through the wall as an annoying noise. On the downside, cast iron is very heavy, expensive and vulnerable to corrosion from acids or very soft water. The hubs in hub-and-spigot joints flare out and require extra-wide stud walls or special chases. Finally, cast iron installation requires the specialized skills and equipment of a plumber and is not friendly to do-it-yourselfers.

Figure 7.8 In times past, cast iron piping sections were joined by molten lead poured into the hub of one section. Oakum packed into the joint kept the lead from running down into the pipe (left). Compressible gaskets (center) can be used to substitute for the lead in a hub-and-spigot joint, while gaskets used with steel clamps (right) do away with the space-hogging hub.

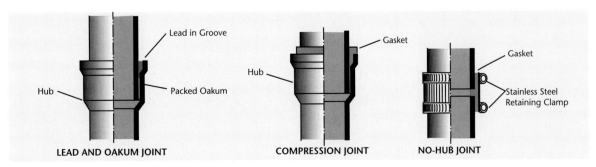

Galvanized Steel

With much the same qualities of cast iron, galvanized steel is accepted by most codes for aboveground DWV piping. Straight sections join together in threaded fittings, as with water supply piping. The material's very high cost and difficult installation rule it out for most projects.

Plastic, the New Kid on the Block

Two types of plastic were introduced in household DWV systems in the 1970s and all but replaced metal piping. **Acrylonitrile-Butadiene-Styrene (ABS)** is a black-colored material first developed for use in oil fields and chemical industries.

Polyvinyl Chloride (PVC) pipe comes in various colors, according to the code-approved use. White is used for household DWV systems. Both materials are lightweight, resistant to chemicals and good up to 180°F (82°C). While not fireproof like cast iron, PVC pipes do self extinguish, rather than burn. Two more pluses make them attractive options. First, they don't flare out much at the fittings, such as a hub on a hub-and-spigot joint in cast iron. So a 3-inch (76 mm) nominal diameter pipe still fits inside a 2x4 studwall.

Second, installation is a snap and can be done by non-plumbers. Pipe sections cut easily with almost any kind of saw. Joints fit together quickly by simply applying the proper solvent cement to the end of the pipe and inside of the fitting, then pushing them together. Sections join to steel pipe with a special connection that has threads for the steel pipe and a solvent-weld connection to the plastic end. Compression gaskets usually join plastic pipe to cast iron pipe.

There are downsides to plastic pipe. Used for the main stack, it transmits the noise of fluids running inside much more than metal. Expansion and contraction under temperatures above 180°F (82°C) may result in joint failure. And runs longer than 30 feet (9,144 mm) must have expansion loops built in to accommodate the expansion/contraction under normal operating temperatures.

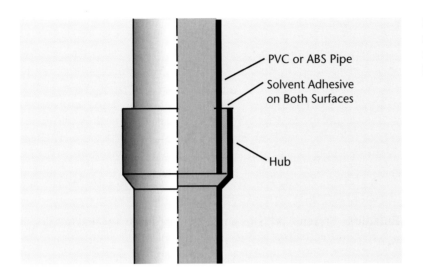

PVC or ABS Pipe

Solvent Adhesive
on Both Surfaces

Hub

Figure 7.9 Plastic pipe is joined by coating both surfaces of the joint with the appropriate solvent, then quickly inserting the pipe into the sleeve.

DWV PIPING MATERIALS AT A GLANCE			
Material	Connections	Pros	Cons
Cast Iron	Lead/oakum, compression clamps	Durable, quiet, resistant to chemicals. Heat resistant and fireproof	Expensive, heavy—requiring structural support, difficult and time consuming to install, corroded by acids
Galvanized Steel	Threaded fittings	Durable, quiet, resistant to chemicals	Most expensive, difficult and time consuming to install, vulnerable to rust
ABS and PVC Plastic	Fittings bonded with ABS or PVC solvent cement	Low cost, lightweight, fast and easy installation	Can be damaged by temperatures above 140°F (60°C), noisy

CHAPTER 8: Plumbing Fixtures, Appliances and Accessories

We began this section on household plumbing with the things clients don't see—the supply and waste systems that serve their fixtures and appliances. But the fixtures, appliances and accessories are what they do see and use, and the reason for those systems hidden in walls and floors.

In this chapter, we'll go over some of the plumbing aspects of fixtures and appliances. You can find more detailed information about selecting the various products themselves from NKBA's *Kitchen & Bath Products* book. Let's begin by defining the various kinds of devices we'll be talking about:

Plumbing Fixtures: Sinks (lavatories, or lavs), toilets, bathtubs, whirlpools, spas and bidets.

Plumbing Appliances: Clothes washers, dishwashers, garbage disposers, water heaters.

Accessories: Controls, valves, drains and fittings.

Plumbing fixtures are constantly changing. Many of the changes are genuine improvements—low-flow toilets that save water come to mind. Some make our lives safer and less complicated. Others, make them more complicated. And manufacturers make many changes to respond to changing lifestyles and consumer tastes. Codes don't usually cover performance of plumbing fixtures and appliances, so it's up to you to acquire the facts on the products you specify from wherever you can.

FIXTURES FOR THE BATH

The bath is probably the most used room in the house, so it's no wonder that it is the most frequently remodeled room. Many of the changes people make when remodeling a bath relate to changes in family make-up and lifestyles. More women working outside the home means baths must accommodate two adults during the peak morning rush hour. Design responses to this can include two lavs, an isolated toilet, maybe a separate tub and shower. People today also want the bath to be something more than a utilitarian space for personal hygiene. Spas for relaxation address this need. But even time-honored utilitarian fixtures, such as toilets, have changed as we'll see.

Lavs

Lavs (also called lavatories, sinks, washbasins and basins) make up the third fixture in the standard three-fixture bath. The other two are a tub or shower and the toilet. Every bathroom needs at least one lavatory and two-person baths increasingly contain two lavs. The days of a single white washbasin hung from the wall or set into a vanity cabinet are long gone. Designers today can choose among a bewildering variety of shapes, sizes, colors and mounting options. Regardless of the type of lav or its installation, the plumbing is separate. Supply piping includes hot and cold water lines. The drain line, typically 1 1/2-inch diameter, leads into a P-trap and horizontal run to the main soil stack. If the distance exceeds 8 feet to 10 feet (2,438 mm to 3,048 mm)—the maximum distance from a fixture to a vent required by most codes—a separate vent (revent) taps off the drain and leads outdoors or to the main stack (see Figure 7.3 in the previous chapter). Fittings include the faucet set and drain.

Toilets

Stroll through a kitchen and bath showroom or thumb through a fixture catalog to see convincing proof that toilets, or "water closets" as they were once called, now come in a bewildering variety of colors, shapes, sizes and styles. Still, the basic function remains the same: getting rid of human waste.

Most toilets do this by using water—a lot of it. They consume more water than any other fixture in the house. Older toilets consumed 5 – 7 gallons (19 L – 26.5 L) for each flush. The U.S. Energy Policy and Conservation Act of 1992 limited the capacity to 1.6 gallons (6 L) for toilets installed after 1994 (at this time there is no such restriction in force in Canada). Consumers complained that low-flow toilets were inefficient, sometimes requiring more than one flush to remove solids. And two or more flushes negated the water-conserving intent. Manufacturers have re-designed the trap-ways of low-flow toilets over the past decade, resulting in improved performance. There are three main types of water-flush toilets currently in use.

Gravity toilets, still the most common type, rely on water from a tank set above the bowl to flush out the contents and refill the trap. Taller, narrower tanks, steeper bowls and smaller water surface areas in the bowl all contribute to improved flushing with less water.

Pressurized tank toilets use the pressure of water in the cold water supply line to compress air, which works with a small amount of water

99

—as little as 0.5 gallons (1.9 L)—to flush the bowl. The higher cost of this type, at least three times as much as a gravity toilet, limits their widespread acceptance. Another drawback is the loud initial sound of the flush that many users have complained about.

Pumped toilets, the most expensive toilet of all, push water through the bowl via a small pump. Pressing a button can set the amount of flush water for 1 or 1.6 gallons (3.8 or 6 L).

Figure 8.1 Gravity toilets rely on water at a higher level to flush out waste in the bowl below. The modern water-saving toilet is the result of several years of evolution, resulting in a fixture that efficiently flushes with only 1.6 gallons of water.

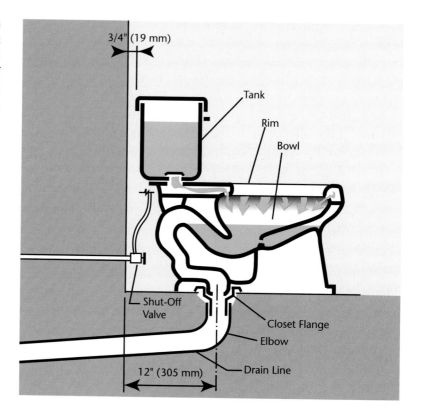

There are two more types of toilets but they are not common in urban or suburban homes. Nevertheless you should be aware of them in the event that you ever design a bath for a vacation house that has no access to a public sewer or septic system. **Incinerating toilets** use electricity to rapidly burn the waste, leaving only an odor-free ash that can be dumped with the household trash. **Composting toilets** work like the compost pile in your backyard to decompose waste. Standard composting toilets sit on the floor like a gravity water toilet and have a composting tank in the basement below. All-in-one units contain a mixer, electric heating element to accelerate composting and a fan to draw odors up the vent. Residue is removed through a cleanout just below the unit.

After specifying a toilet by type and model, be sure to indicate the appropriate rough-in dimensions. Most gravity toilets require a 12 inch (305 mm) dimension from the face of the framing to the centerline of the drain hole, however this assumes a wall finish material no thicker than 1/2 inch (13 mm). The added thickness of a wood wainscot will require a corresponding addition to the rough-in dimensions. Also, some toilets are made for 10-inch (254 mm) and 14-inch (356 mm) rough-ins.

TOILETS IN THE BASEMENT

If a house sits into a hillside, its waste line may be below the basement floor slab. A toilet can then be installed in the standard way, with its drain below the slab. But in most houses the main waste line runs under the first floor and out through the foundation. A toilet installed in the basement is too low to flush by gravity. The answer is an ejector pump that grinds the solid waste and pumps it up into the house waste line. The typical installation uses a standard gravity toilet mounted on the slab. It drains into an ejector pump that sits inside a tank below the slab. Flushing the toilet raises the level of the waste fluid in the tank which triggers the pump switch to suck in the waste, grind the solids into a slurry and pump the mixture up through a 2-inch diameter pipe into the waste line. A separate vent pipe must run from the tank up through the house and exit to the outdoors. Units that combine toilet with ejector pump are also available. In these, both the toilet and the pump sit on a platform above the slab, eliminating the need to tear into the slab.

Bidets

Bidets are one of the least understood fixtures of the bathroom. Common in Europe, bidets are more and more in demand in high-end baths in North American homes as a cleansing fixture for the pelvic area. A bidet looks something like a toilet with no tank or lid and usually sits beside the toilet. The user sits astride the bidet facing the wall, to cleanse the pelvic area using warm water sprayed from the back of the unit. There is also a vertical spray model with controls at the back and a water inlet in the bowl bottom. Both a hot and cold water supply are required, as well as a drain. Vertical spray models include a vacuum breaker, since the water comes in below the flood level of the fixture.

Figure 8.2 When toilets are installed below the waste line of the house, they must be hooked up to an ejector pump that grinds the waste into slurry and pumps it up to the waste line. The device can be mounted in a pit below the floor, as shown, or set behind the toilet, if the toilet is installed on a platform above the floor.

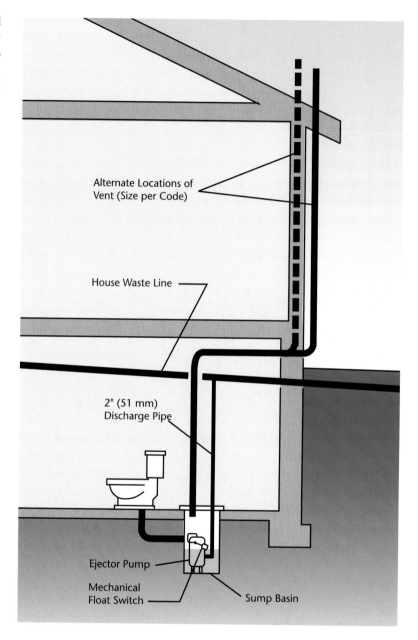

Alternate Locations of
Vent (Size per Code)

House Waste Line

2" (51 mm)
Discharge Pipe

Ejector Pump

Mechanical
Float Switch

Sump Basin

Bathtubs and Tub/Showers

Many people seldom or never use bathtubs, preferring the speed and convenience of a shower for full-body cleansing. Tub/showers combine both, but while the shower above a tub saves space, it is not as convenient as a separate shower stall. In any case, it's probably a good idea for every house to have at least one tub. Babies, small children and some elderly persons can't use showers. A bathtub is still considered a necessary asset when it comes time to resell the house.

Tubs are available as the tub only. When you specify a tub installation, you must also indicate which fittings it is to have. All tubs need a drain/overflow assembly. Hot- and cold-water faucets can be separate or combined into a single-lever control with an integral anti-scald device. If a shower is part of the assembly, you will also need to specify the type of showerhead.

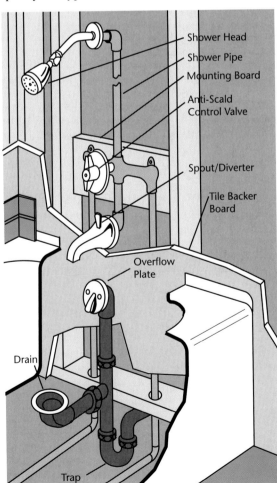

Figure 8.3 Fittings and installation for a typical tub/shower unit.

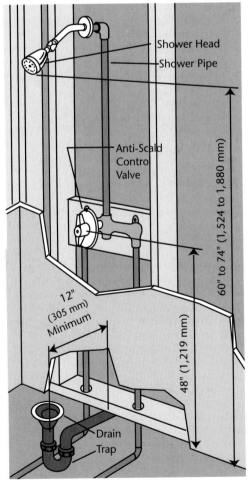

Figure 8.4 Fittings and installation for a typical shower.

Shower Stalls

As with lavs and tubs, the plumbing is separate and basically the same as described for tubs, except that there is no spout at the tub level and the controls are at a height reachable while standing. Fittings inside the shower include dual faucets or a single control, a showerhead and drain fitting. Showerheads may be mounted in a fixed position or on a flexible hose that allows the head to be handheld to direct the spray as desired (this type is preferred for persons who must sit while showering).

Luxury Showers

For homeowners with a taste for the exotic and budget to pay for it, there is a whole world of amenities that expand the capabilities of showers beyond the simple spout mounted on the wall. Manufacturers now offer water delivery systems that spray the whole body by arrays of jets on the wall. Some have pumps that recirculate the water from a reservoir in the base. The user showers first to cleanse the body, then drains the dirty water and refills the basin with fresh water that recirculates as a massage as in a stand-up whirlpool. Other models include the steam of a Turkish bath or dry heat of a sauna. Tanning lamps and warm breezes are other features available. We couldn't cover all the possibilities in this book (they change too rapidly anyway), so your best source for information is manufacturers' catalogs.

Whirlpools and Spas

Like bidets, whirlpools and spas are increasingly popular. Their appeal is their ability to relax people stressed out from the pressures of modern life. **Whirlpools** are basically bathtubs with jets around the bottom to circulate warm water under the pressure of a pump. As bathing fixtures, they are drained after each use. **Spas** evolved from hot tubs and are basically vessels for soaking, not bathing. They are not drained after each use and users should be clean when they enter the spa.

Regardless of their heritage, spas today contain the same water-circulation equipment as whirlpools. Both require the same supply and drainage plumbing as described for lavs, tubs and showers, with two exceptions. First, spas often contain their own water heater, which eliminates the need for a hot water line. Second, though 1/2-inch supply piping will work fine for whirlpools—especially if their main use is for bathing in shallow water—a 3/4-inch pipe will fill the unit quicker, so is recommended for spas and for whirlpools intended primarily for soaking.

The pump circulates water in a whirlpool or spa. Located under or adjacent to the unit, it must remain accessible via a panel at the side, front or rear. After selecting the unit, make sure you provide electrical service required by the manufacturer's specifications. Pumps are typically 1.5 or 2 hp, requiring a dedicated electrical circuit of 15 or 20-amp capacity and a switch protected with a ground fault circuit interrupter (GFCI) device.

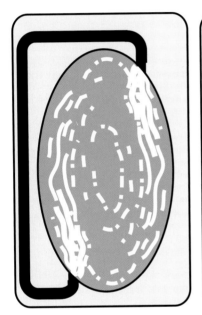 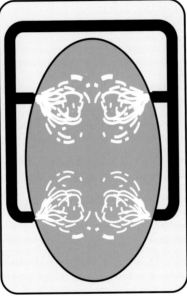

Figure 8.5 True whirlpool tubs jet the water into a whirlpool pattern, as shown at left. However this is just one option. Other units create different patterns of turbulence by varying the arrangement of the nozzles.

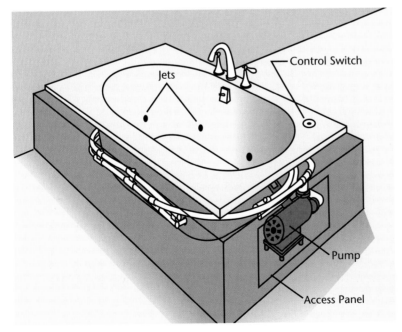

Figure 8.6 Whirlpools and spas typically mount on framed platforms. A removable panel must always be provided to access the pump.

KITCHEN EQUIPMENT

Kitchens today are the center of family life and often the focus of home entertaining. Both men and women use them. The guests may even pitch in. Kitchens are both places for preparing full meals and eat-on-the-run snacks. And that's not all. Today's kitchens must also include provisions for recycling and perhaps even a home office space. As a kitchen designer, you must accommodate all these demands with innovative design schemes. You will find a wide variety of state-of-the-art fixtures and appliances to help you with this challenge.

Sinks

Kitchen sink choices are as varied as lavs for bathrooms, except for mounting options, since they most always mount on or under a countertop. The current trend is for more than one sink in a kitchen to enable two people to work at the same time. However, the second sink will more likely be for a special purpose, such as washing vegetables. Sinks not connected to a disposer typically include a strainer to keep food scraps out of the drainage piping. If there is a disposer below, a stopper fits into the drain and is removed to allow food scraps into the disposer.

The plumbing for a sink not equipped with a disposer is pretty much the same as for a lav, as was described above, but the fittings differ. Gooseneck spouts that swivel between sinks are an oft-chosen option. A separate spray hose is fairly standard. Various types of water filter devices can connect to the cold water supply either under the sink or topside.

Figure 8.7 Typical installation of a disposer. Note that when installed below a double sink, the disposer is located below the bowl farthest away from the drain line.

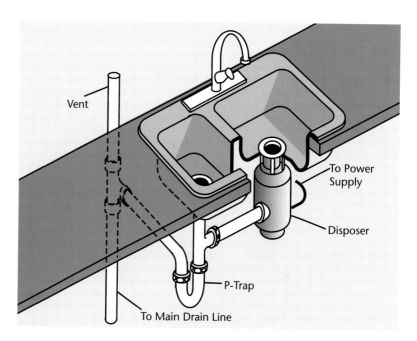

Disposers connect to the drain under the sink (to the main drain, in the case of a double sink). They are powered from a 120v outlet under the sink. **Continuous-feed disposers** are wired to a switch under the countertop or to a GFCI-protected switch above the countertop. Turning the switch activates the motor in the disposer. **Batch-feed disposers** operate intermittently whenever the user turns the lid in the sink to the open position.

Dishwashers

A luxury yesterday, dishwashers are considered basic equipment in kitchens of today. Most dishwashers are built into the base cabinet area, under or adjacent to the sink. Plumbing rough-in must be in place before the unit is installed and includes a 3/8-inch hot water line, copper tubing preferred, which enters the dishwasher's space from the side or rear of the base cabinets. The drain rises up the back or side of the dishwasher to connect to the tailpiece of the sink drain by a special "dishwasher tee." Some codes require an air gap fitting on the high end of the waste hose loop to prevent siphoning. The air gap assembly mounts on the countertop above the rim of the sink. Some sinks have an extra hole near the faucet assembly for this purpose.

There are also portable models designed to sit outside the cabinetry, but to install below the countertop if the homeowner decides to renovate. They need no built-in plumbing. The hot water supply hose from the unit simply snaps onto the sink faucet and the drain hose hangs over the sink. Their inconvenience makes these models more suitable for a temporary kitchen, or one in transition, than a permanent one.

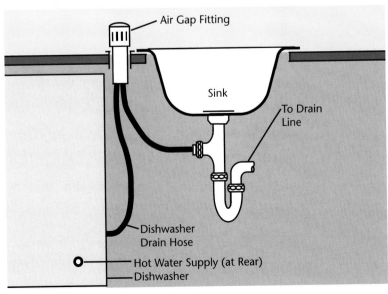

Figure 8.8 A dishwasher typically mounts under the countertop next to the sink, so that the drain hose from the dishwasher can connect into the trap from the sink. Some codes require an air gap fitting on the high end of the waste hose loop to prevent siphoning.

Other Fixtures that Require Plumbing Connections

As kitchen fixtures and appliances evolve, manufacturers add features that may require more than a simple connection to the plumbing system. When you specify appliances, check the manufacturer's technical specifications thoroughly to obtain the installation requirements, then specify all necessary plumbing provisions in your plans. Refrigerators equipped to supply filtered cold water or ice cubes need a cold water supply line, typically a 1/4-inch copper tube from the back wall. Water purification devices installed in the kitchen can mount above or under the countertop. They usually connect to the cold water supply line with a flexible hose from the device, but consult the manufacturer's data for the plumbing requirements.

PART FOUR: ELECTRICAL SYSTEMS

No modern kitchen or bath can function without electricity. You can expect the electrician on the job to know how to circuit and wire the electrical fixtures you specify. For your part, you will need a basic understanding of two areas: 1) the power system and 2) kitchen and bath lighting. We'll cover the basics of both areas in the final part of this book.

CHAPTER 9: Home Electrical Power Systems

Let's begin by defining some of the terms you will deal with in household electrical systems. We'll risk some scientific accuracy in the interest of making them easier to understand.

Electrical current is the flow of electrons over conductors. There are two types of current flow. In **Alternating Current (AC)**, the type of current used in household wiring, the current changes polarity, or alternates, continually from positive to negative and back again at the rate of 60 times a second. **Direct Current (DC)** is steady-state flow, in which the positive and negative wires retain the same polarity. Batteries supply DC current.

We measure the quantity of current flow in units called **amperes**, or **amps**, abbreviated as "**a**". Electrical current needs a force to push the electrons along the line. This force is called **voltage** and is measured in **volts (v)**. Voltage is necessary because the wires that conduct electricity are not perfect conductors. Their resistance varies with the type of metal. Copper offers very little resistance, while the tungsten wires inside light bulbs offer a lot—so much, in fact, that much of the energy intended for light gets wasted as heat. **Resistance** is measured in **Ohms**. We have **electrical power**, measured in **watts (W)**, when there is a certain voltage available to force current through a conductor. The power formula tells how much power:

$$\text{Power} = \text{voltage x amperage, or } W = VA$$

Voltage and/or amperage ratings are typically listed for each electrical device in the manufacturer's specifications, so you can determine the power requirements to provide on the circuit. If the amperage isn't given, you can find it by varying the formula and plugging in the known values. For example, if you wanted to find out how many amps a 120w exhaust fan consumes on a 120v circuit,

$$A = W/A = 120/60 = 2.$$

Another formula, **Ohm's Law**, states the relationship between volts, amps and resistance (ohms):

$$\text{Amps} = \text{volts/ohms}$$

This second formula tells us why lights and appliances may draw different amounts of current (amps) even when connected to the same voltage source.

THE SERVICE ENTRANCE

Electricity enters the home from the transformer on the nearest power pole. The transformer reduces the voltage to 240v for household use. A supply cable connects the transformer with the **electric meter** in the home via an overhead or underground service cable. This cable then continues into the home to the main **service panel**, or "distribution central," for the household electrical systems. At the entry point to the panel the service cable contains three wires or conductors. Two are "live" or "hot," insulated with black plastic. The third is a "neutral," or "grounded," bare copper or aluminum wire (actually a bundle of small wires). The two hot wires carry a potential of 240 volts between the two conductors. The potential voltage for a device wired to one hot wire and the neutral wire is 120v.

Figure 9.1 Electrical power comes into the home from the transformer on the nearest power pole via overhead or underground cables. After passing through the meter, enters the main service panel, which then distributes power to various circuits.

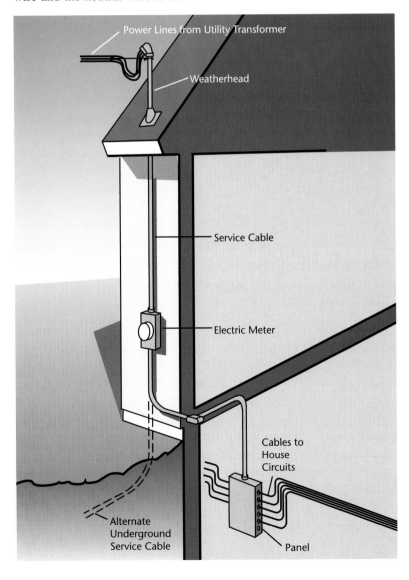

Inside the Service Panel

The three conductors from the service cable connect to the **main breaker**, a combination shutoff switch and overload protecting device for the entire home. The main breaker connects to flat bars called **buses** that run down inside the panel. **Circuit breakers** for individual household circuits snap onto the buses to tap off 240v or 120v power, according to whether they connect to two hot buses (water heaters, for example) or a hot plus neutral bus, in the case of household appliances that draw 120v. An electrical circuit is a path of electrons from the power source from a hot wire, through an appliance or device, back to the power source through the neutral, or grounded, conductor, as shown in Figure 9.2.

Figure 9.2 All electrical circuits require a power source, a positive (hot) wire, a negative (neutral) wire, an appliance that draws current and a switch to control the flow of electricity through the circuit.

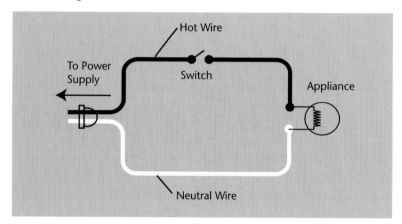

Circuit breakers protect branch circuits from electrical overloads or shorts in the circuit. Without this protection, the excess electrical energy would turn to heat and eventually melt the wiring insulation and ignite any combustible material nearby.

Older houses may have a panel box equipped with **fuses** rather than circuit breakers. Fuses contain a thin metal strip that snaps apart when the circuit is overloaded, breaking the circuit. Main breakers are usually a cartridge type that plugs into the terminals. Fuses for branch circuits are typically glass and screw in to sockets in the fuse box. Once the fuse blows, it must be replaced. Homeowners lacking spare fuses sometimes stuck a penny behind a glass blown fuse, risking an electrical fire. Because of this hazard and the fact that fuses had to be replaced every time they were triggered, they were replaced by circuit breakers. Depending on the size of the house, the panel should have at least a 100a capacity main breaker and likely a 200a one. A qualified electrician is the person to consult on this question.

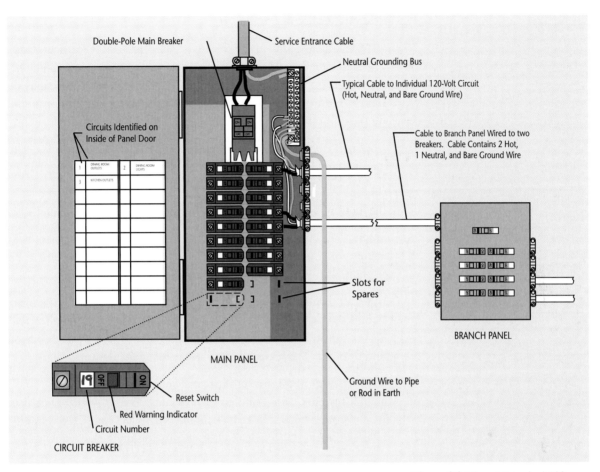

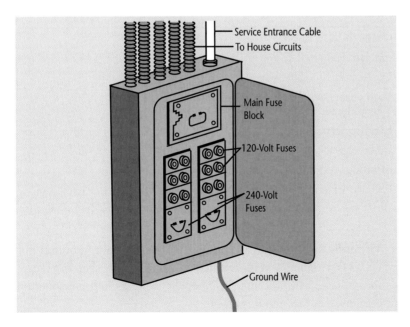

Figure 9.3 (above) A typical 100-amp main service entrance panel. Remodeling or additions may require more new circuits than are available as spares, so a branch panel is added, tapping off two breakers in the main panel.

Figure 9.4 (left) Fuse boxes are often found in older houses. Because fuses must be replaced each time they are overloaded, this system can be a nuisance and unsafe (EX: if someone places a penny behind a blown fuse instead of replacing it). A fuse box can be replaced with a panel containing circuit breakers.

Household Circuits

Panels configured to conform to the National Electrical Code (U.S.) contain four types of circuits: general lighting, small appliance, individual appliance and ground fault circuit interrupter. There may be one or more of each type, depending on the size of the house and number of appliances.

General lighting circuits serve lighting and wall receptacles. The code requires 3 watts per square foot of living area, the equivalent of one 15a circuit for each 600 square feet (55.74 m²) or one 20a circuit per 800 square feet (73.32 m²). A rule of thumb for the number of receptacles allots 12 outlets for 15a circuits and 16 outlets for 30a circuits. The code also requires a light controlled by a permanent wall switch for each room. **Lights in kitchens and baths must be permanently wired** rather than plug-in type.

Small appliance circuits serve receptacles for plug-in appliances such as toasters, blenders and coffee makers. The code requires two 20a circuits in the kitchen and one or more in the pantry and dining or family rooms. These circuits may not be used for lighting.

Individual appliance circuits are dedicated to devices that draw enough current to warrant their own circuits. The following table lists some of the candidates that may occur in kitchens and baths. Always verify the manufacturer's electrical requirements for appliances you specify.

Appliance	Voltage	Breaker Capacity, Amps
Garbage Disposer	120	20
Electric Range or Cooktop	240	50
Gas Range or Cooktop	120	20
Dishwasher with Water Heater Included	120	20
Electric Tankless Water Heater	240	30
Refrigerator	120	20
Microwave Oven	120	20
Exhaust Fan	120	20

Ground fault circuit interrupters (GFCI) are required for receptacles within 6 feet (1,829 mm) of a water source, such as a faucet or showerhead. Most receptacles mounted above a kitchen countertop or bath lavatory fall into this category.

Adding Circuits

Service panels in new houses should include several spare, or blank, spaces below the installed circuit breakers to enable the homeowner to add circuits in the future. Remodeling or additions usually require added circuits. What do you do if the panel has no spares? There are three possibilities:

1. If the existing panel is outdated, such as a fuse box type, it's a good idea replace the entire panel with an updated one with adequate capacity for both the existing and additional loads.

2. If the panel is adequate, but simply lacks spare slots, you can replace standard branch circuit breakers with "mini" breakers, which are half as thick as standard breakers, so that two minis fit into one slot intended for a standard-width breaker (The NEC, article 408.15, limits the total number of breakers in any one panel to 42).

3. A branch panel might be added, piggyback, to the main panel.

Consult the electrician on the project for the best way to obtain sufficient new circuits.

WIRE AND CONDUITS

Electrical current travels via two types of conductors on its way from panel to appliance: cables and cords. Cables are the "hard wiring" in houses. They run from the circuit breakers to junction boxes in the walls (or floors). A cord with a plug connects portable appliances to receptacles in the boxes. Hard-wired appliances (those not portable) connect to the cable in junction boxes by wires rather than cords.

A **cable** has two or more wires bundled inside a protective sheathing of plastic or metal. The most common cable for residential wiring is **nonmetallic sheathed cable**, known as **Romex**, which bundles together a single hot wire encased in black plastic, a white-encased neutral wire and a bare ground wire—all wrapped inside an insulating plastic sheath. A **cord**, a flexible conductor of stranded wire, contains two or three separate conductors insulated from each other by rubber or plastic.

Another type of cable is contained within a flexible metal sheathing. **Armored (BX)** cable is sometimes specified for uses needing extra sheathing protection. BX cable is restricted to indoor use in dry locations.

Copper is the material of choice today in residential wiring. Aluminum gained some popularity in the 1960s and 1970s, as a more economical alternative. It fell from grace when its tendency to expand and contract when heated and cooled made it pull away from terminal screws, breaking the connection and causing an arc—a potential fire hazard. While it is still used for some wiring from the meter to the panel, its use is discouraged for branch circuit wiring. If you encounter aluminum wiring on any branch circuits you may be dealing with, it should be replaced with copper or, if this is not feasible, make sure any switches or outlets connected to the circuit are rated for aluminum wiring.

Wire Size

Wire is sized by **gauge**. The larger the gauge, the smaller the wire diameter. Wire gauges in North America are based on the American Wire Gauge (AWG) system, which expresses the size as a whole number. Most household cable uses 12- or 14-gauge wire (14 gauge is the smallest permitted by code, except for low-voltage circuits, such as thermostats and doorbells). Circuits for 120v appliances and lighting typically use 12-gauge wiring. The wire connecting a device with a switch may be 14-gauge. But these are only generalizations. In actuality, the current that the wire must carry determines its size. An undersized wire risks overheating and fire. A 12-gauge wire is rated to carry a maximum of 20 amps. A 14-gauge wire is rated for up to 15 amps.

The size and other traits appear on the outer wrap of cable and wire in abbreviated form. For example, consider the following identifying markings on a Romex cable:

12/2 WITH GROUND, TYPE NMC, 600V (UL)

The first number, 12, is the gauge. The second indicates that there are two conductors. "WITH GROUND" tells us that there is a separate ground wire. The type, NMC, means it is nonmetallic cable. Finally, the maximum safe voltage capacity of the cable is given, with the testing agency, Underwriters Laboratories.

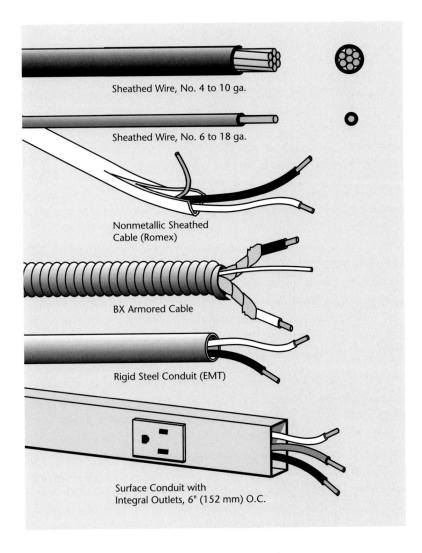

Sheathed Wire, No. 4 to 10 ga.

Sheathed Wire, No. 6 to 18 ga.

Nonmetallic Sheathed
Cable (Romex)

BX Armored Cable

Rigid Steel Conduit (EMT)

Surface Conduit with
Integral Outlets, 6" (152 mm) O.C.

Figure 9.5 Many types of wire and cable are available to meet the needs of any project. The gauge and type of cable is noted on the package and/or on the cable itself. Nonmetallic sheathed cable (Romex) is used in most housing circuits. Surface-mounted conduit (bottom) with outlets spaced 6" (152 mm) apart is a good way to ensure enough outlets where they are needed above kitchen countertops.

Conduit and Raceways

Whereas cable is an all-in-one wiring conductor, conduit is a protective sleeve that is installed before the conductors are inserted. Its use in residential wiring occurs mainly outside the house. Service cable from the street to the house is often buried in PVC plastic conduit. Aboveground conduit is typically light-duty **electrical metallic tubing (EMT)**, made of thin-walled galvanized steel. EMT conduit comes in diameters of 1/2 inch to 1 1/4 inches.

Another type of conduit, a **raceway**, mounts on the wall surface. It enables running cable from one place to another without fishing it through the insides of walls, a boon on remodeling projects.

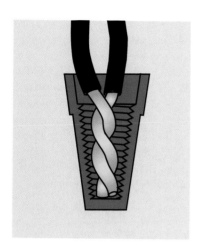

Figure 9.6 Plastic wire nuts are a quick way to join wires. They come in various sizes and colors. Codes do not permit connections outside of accessible junction boxes.

Wiring Devices

Various accessories called wiring devices complete the electrical system. All wiring systems require a means of connecting wires to each other. The code requires all electrical connections to occur inside a junction box. The most common connector for household wiring is a **wire nut**, a simple plastic cap that screws over the ends of two or more wires, forming a twisted connection inside, while insulating the outside. Wire nuts come in various sizes and colors.

Junction boxes are simple round, octagonal or rectangular containers that house the terminal points of wires and serve as access points for devices. All switches and receptacles must be contained within code-approved junction boxes. Boxes made of galvanized steel and plastic are manufactured in various sizes to fit the number of connections made inside. They can be nailed to the side or face of studs or ceiling joists. Your design drawings should locate all junction boxes that contain switches or outlets. The NKBA recommends that wall receptacles be located between 15 inches and 48 inches (381 mm – 1,219 mm) above the finished floor.

Switches control electricity to appliances by turning it on or off or by adjusting the voltage level. The most familiar on-off switch is the **single-pole toggle switch** that you flip up or down. Other types gaining favor include **rocker switches**, controlled by pushing against the top or bottom of the rocker plate and **plate switches**, controlled by pushing the entire plate in. Switches other than the single-pole type suit other needs. A **three-way switch** allows the user to turn a hall lamp on *and* off from either end of the hall. It is also useful mounted next to a bed, so that the person can turn lights off after getting into bed. Sometimes you may need to control a device from three locations. Simply specify a **four-way switch**. Wiring for a three- and four-way switch gets complicated, but a competent electrician will know how to install it correctly.

Appliances that run off 240 volts typically need **double-pole switches**, which have four, rather than two, terminals as with a single-pole switch.

Dimmer switches with rotary knobs or sliding levers are increasingly popular for some lighting circuits, particularly in living, dining and bedroom lighting. Pushing the knob in turns the device on or off. Turning it adjusts the voltage up or down to control the desired level of lighting.

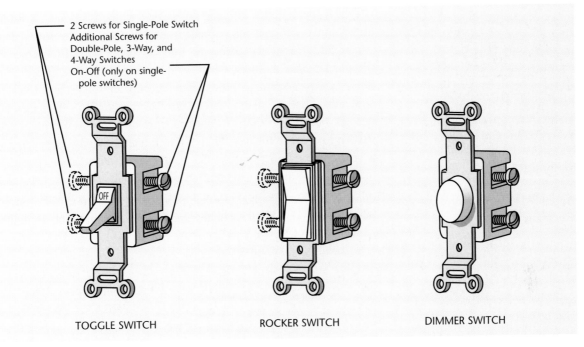

2 Screws for Single-Pole Switch
Additional Screws for
Double-Pole, 3-Way, and
4-Way Switches
On-Off (only on single-
pole switches)

OFF

TOGGLE SWITCH   ROCKER SWITCH   DIMMER SWITCH

Receptacles vary by their intended use. The most common type for household circuits running on 120 volts is a **duplex receptacle** with two outlets. Each outlet has two side-by-side slots for the hot and neutral prongs of the cord and a semi-round slot below for the ground prong. Two-slot ungrounded receptacles found in older houses are no longer acceptable by the code. A special type receptacle with a slot configuration that prevents a 120v device from being plugged into it is used for 240v appliances. The top portion of duplex receptacles in living rooms and bedrooms are often connected to switches, so the user can plug lamps into them, but are all controlled from one switch.

The code requirement that receptacles located within 6 feet (1,829 mm) of a moisture source is a problem to deal with for receptacles in baths or kitchens, particularly for receptacles mounted above countertops. The best solution is to protect the entire circuit with a **ground fault circuit interrupter (GFCI)** circuit breaker at the main service panel. If this can't be done, the next best is a **GFCI receptacle**, which has a reset button to turn the power back on after any problem that triggers it has been fixed. The kitchen and bath industry suggests a single GFCI receptacle in the kitchen or bath, wired to other receptacles down-line from it. A third solution is a GFCI receptacle that plugs into an unprotected receptacle. Though the most economical, this fix is not the most elegant and risks easy removal by anyone who may not like its appearance.

Figure 9.7 Switches can be on-off (first two examples, left to right) or variable (dimmer) to control various devices and circuits. A single-pole switch has two terminals to control a single circuit. A three-way switch has three terminals, one marked "COM." It controls a circuit from two places. Double-pole switches with four terminals control 240v appliances. Four-way switches also have four terminals. They are used to control a device from three locations.

119

Figure 9.8 (below) The number, shape, size, and configuration of the slots in receptacles determine the type of circuit and amperage they connect to.

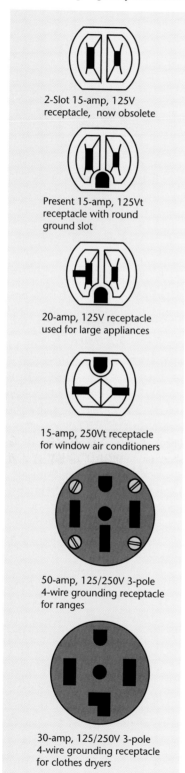

2-Slot 15-amp, 125V receptacle, now obsolete

Present 15-amp, 125Vt receptacle with round ground slot

20-amp, 125V receptacle used for large appliances

15-amp, 250Vt receptacle for window air conditioners

50-amp, 125/250V 3-pole 4-wire grounding receptacle for ranges

30-amp, 125/250V 3-pole 4-wire grounding receptacle for clothes dryers

The code requires receptacles to be located such that a 6-foot (1,829 mm) cord can reach them from any point in the room. This works pretty well for baths, as long as there are GFCI-protected receptacles near the lavs, where shaving and hair drying occur. But kitchens never seem to have enough receptacles for the variety of appliances that use them. Aim to provide receptacles where they are needed, but don't skimp. If you can't provide an outlet every 2 feet (610 mm) or so in the back wall of the countertop, consider specifying a surface-mounted raceway that has integral receptacles spaced at intervals of 12 inches (305 mm). Since peninsulas have no back wall for receptacles, it is best to mount them on a side wall, where they are out of danger of water splashing into them and causing a short circuit.

Figure 9.9 (right) Codes require ground fault circuit interrupter (GFCI) outlets in any location near water, such as a sink or lav, to protect against electrocution. A standard outlet connected to a GFCI breaker in the panel may be substituted for a GFCI outlet.

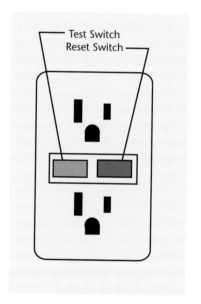

Test Switch
Reset Switch

Solving Remodeling Woes

Wiring a new house or addition is a snap compared to wiring a renovation. The electrician has to make your plan work, but the more you know about the pitfalls and solutions, the smoother the installation will be.

The first snag may arise when you discover that the home's service panel doesn't have any spare slots for additional circuit breakers (the spares will be blank spaces in the circuit breaker array). If the panel is an outdated fuse box, it probably should be replaced with a newer one with enough capacity. If it is up-to-date, but lacks spare slots, a branch panel might be piggybacked onto it for the new circuits.

Getting wires to the outlets and switches can be thorny, particularly with plaster walls. The electrician might be able to "fish" them through walls by cutting holes near the floor and ceiling, then using a fish-tape tool to pull the wires through the cavities. Running the wires horizontally may require removing all or part of the wall finish so the wires can be run through holes in the studs, as with new construction. **Any wires run through notches cut into the face of studs must be covered with a metal plate to protect the wires from puncture by nails or screws.** Each project is different, so you should visit the site to size-up the situation early on in your design.

Re-use of existing junction boxes can pose another obstacle. A box may be too shallow for the new switch or outlet or too small for the number of wires that it must accommodate. Replacing the box with a new one entails some demolition and it may be easier to gut the entire wall finish than try to attempt a cut-and-patch job at the problem box. Or, if the design allows the outlet or switch to protrude beyond the face of the wall, a **box extension** can add the required depth.

The wiring system and devices mentioned so far make up the bulk of electrical systems in North American homes. But they may not be the only option for the future. A revolution in electronic technology during the past two decades spawned some mind-boggling developments that are bound to change or at least expand the capabilities of household electrical systems, as we'll see in the following sections.

LOW-VOLTAGE WIRING SYSTEMS

Standard home wiring meets the needs of devices that operate off of 120 volts or higher. But thermostats, doorbells, speakers and telephones run on very low line voltage that requires small-diameter wires or cables. The spate of new electronic technologies in recent years has created the need for specially designed low-voltage wiring systems that are completely separate from the electrical power network of the home.

Low-Voltage Lighting

Halogen lamps are becoming an increasingly popular alternative to incandescent lamps. In addition to lamps that work off standard 120v circuits, there are halogen lamps for low-voltage applications that draw 12 volts supplied by a transformer. Most low-voltage fixtures, such as recessed ceiling lights and track lights, include built-in transformers. Where a fixture is too small to accommodate a transformer, lights can be grouped together and served by a remote transformer that may be installed in an out-of-the-way location such as under a wall cabinet. Expect a device about the size of a pound of butter. One example of this is a series of shallow puck lights mounted under a wall cabinet above a kitchen countertop. The wiring that supplies the transformer is the same as that used in other 120v household circuits.

Structured Wiring

The low-voltage wire that serves so well for the doorbell and telephone is woefully inadequate for computers and high-definition TV sets, as well as a host of other new electronic devices and some we don't even know about yet. Internet service slows to a crawl on standard telephone cable. Structured wiring handles these needs and offers many more possibilities, such as linking multiple telephone and fax lines and high-speed modems. It enables computers in different rooms to talk to each other, as well as to printers and other peripheral devices.

A structured wiring system consists of a network of special cables that make home runs from ports in the walls of various rooms to a central panel, located in a closet somewhere. The ports typically mount near power wiring receptacles and include outlets that fit the jacks of devices to be plugged into them. A port might, for example, contain a phone jack, a data jack and a TV jack. Structured wiring requires two basic types of cable: **Category 5 (cat 5)** cable, a blend of four insulated wire pairs twisted to minimize interference and **coaxial cable, type RG 6**, a single wire encased within a woven wire sheath. Cat 5 cable comes in several versions, cat 5e (enhanced) can handle four phone or data lines, with many times the bandwidth capacity of bell wire. For locations that require both cat 5 and RG 6, such as a living room with a high-definition TV, there is a single cable that bundles both together.

The structured wiring panel is the "brain" of the system that gives structured wiring its flexibility. Terminals here enable a computer in one room to print on a printer in another, or a VCR in the living room to send a movie to a bedroom TV. One cable carries the signal to the TV and one carries instructions from a remote sensor back to the VCR. The homeowner can rearrange the communication between various connected devices by rearranging the connections in the panel.

Structured wiring is sensitive to interference from the home power wiring and should be installed after the primary wiring, with a minimum separation of 6 inches (152 mm) between itself and any 120v or 240v lines.

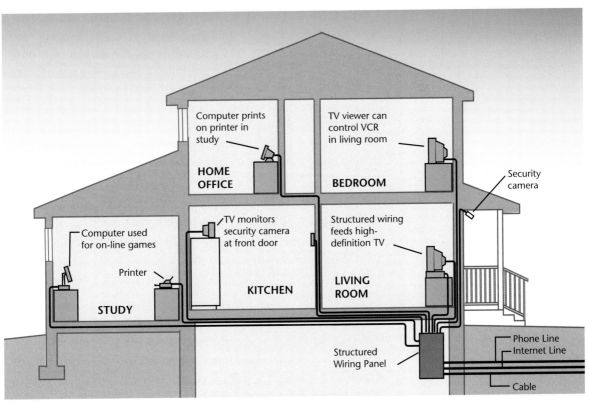

Figure 9.10 (above) Structured wiring links various electronic devices in a home, enabling them to communicate with each other and to accept automated control. The nerve center of the system is the structured wiring panel, where wires from the whole house come together, enabling future changes in the arrangement of devices and the system.

Figure 9.11 (left) Tech ports (left) installed in each room accept various types of device cables. Category 5e (cat 5e) cable (right), the current favorite in structured wiring systems, contains four wire pairs that terminate in an RJ 45 jack. Wires are color coded by an industry standard.

HOME AUTOMATION SYSTEMS

The "house of the future" has been the dream of designers and manufacturers for years and versions have cropped up at every World's Fair. Past concepts envisioned appliances that functioned automatically, anticipating our every need; robots that relieved us of household drudgery and other wonders. Until the 1980s, most of these ideas remained mere dreams, then several major participants in the housing, large appliance and electrical control industries pursued the idea of integrating home automation into a system that would monitor and operate lighting, heating, cooling, ventilation, appliances, entertainment and security devices.

The drive toward home automation took shape in 1984 under the label **"smart house,"** a package for new homes conceived by the National Association of Home Builders (NAHB). Research and development have continued by an offshoot of that project called the Smart House Limited Partnership, which sells a complete wiring system for new construction.

Several approaches have since resulted, which enable the homeowner to program, control, or monitor the house by a computer or even by telephone. Some type of home automation system presently serves an estimated 5 million homes, but the market is growing, spurred on by the increasing number of digital technologies available to consumers today. Since home automation systems affect every electrical appliance in the kitchen and bath, as a designer, you should be familiar with the approaches currently available.

Types of Systems

There are three types of home automation controls.

Centrally Controlled Communication Systems

Centrally controlled communication systems route signals between a central computer and appliance controllers or environmental sensors. These systems can control some "dumb" appliances as well as "smart" appliances. If the controller fails, however, the whole system fails. The major distinction in "smart" home technology is the way electricity is distributed throughout the home.

A central control system allots incoming household electricity to a distribution unit in each room of the house. The distribution unit (or network box) does not provide power to the outlets in the room indiscriminately, as in a conventional home. The new outlets contain microprocessor chips that only provide power upon request by a "smart" appliance. "Smart" appliances have microprocessor chips that enable them to communicate their identity, power demands and functional status to the network box when the appliance is plugged in. If the computer system determines that all is well, the network box sends power to that outlet. If the network senses potential danger, such as a frayed cord, or appliance incompatibility, the system denies power to the outlet. An outlet is only live when utilized by a compatible appliance.

Distributed-Control Systems

Distributed-control systems use wiring already in the home, such as standard power line wiring, telephone wire (4 pair), video wire (dual coaxial), radio frequency (RF) signals and infrared (IR) signals. Microchip controls installed in appliances or outlets enable individual appliances to communicate with each other over the existing electrical wiring without a central controller, although keyboard entry is possible using telephones or personal computers. The system's status can be monitored on the home TV set. Compatible appliances are necessary, but there is no standard in place at this time to make them so. To achieve a common standard, the Electronic Industries Association has developed a standard communications protocol, CEBus, which will allow appliances and modems from different manufacturers to communicate with each other. Individual semiconductor manufacturers have developed microchips that could be installed in appliances.

Individual Control Devices

Individual control devices are the simplest and most economical home automation system. Devices control single appliances or functions, such as programmable setback thermostats, motion detectors, occupancy sensors, photocell lighting controls and timers. These systems can also be applied to applications ranging from outdoor lighting to security sensors. The familiar television remote may come to mind, but it's not truly a home automation device, since it requires the user's conscious thought and effort to operate.

ELECTRICITY FROM THE SUN

We live in the space age and profit from advances made in its research. One of the spin-off technologies that benefit homes came with the development of **photovoltaics (PV)**, a means of converting sunlight directly into electrical energy. Conceived in 1950 for space applications, PV systems now provide thousands of houses with some or all of their electricity. The technology is clean, quiet, reliable and friendly to the environment. What's more, it lessens dependency on public electricity, which continues to rise in price.

Of course, all of this comes with a price that exceeds the installed cost of a standard wiring system for most houses. At the present time, PV systems are most cost-effective for rural sites remote from a utility power source and for houses located with a lot of sunshine, year-round, such as the southwestern U.S. Still, constant improvements in the technology over the last 20 years continue to reduce the installed cost of PV systems, making them a more attractive option to a greater number of homeowners.

The key to a photovoltaic system is a silicon cell made of a silicon semi-conducting material, the same kind of material from which computer chips are made. When developing the computer chip, engineers found that the electrical output in the computer chip would change when exposed to light. This became known as the photovoltaic effect. When sunlight strikes a PV cell, it knocks an electron loose, creating an electrical current. Tiny wires embedded in the PV cell collect that electricity. Because each PV cell produces just a small amount of electricity, a number of PV cells need to be hooked together into a PV panel, or array, to produce enough electricity for a household. A 100-square-foot (9.3-square-meter) PV system will generate a peak power of about 1 kW, energy enough to meet many power requirements of an average U.S. home.

PV panels typically mount on a south-facing roof. They feed direct current (DC) to an inverter that converts the DC power to alternating current (AC), so it can be used with standard household appliances. Because the sun's energy varies with the time of day and sky conditions, PV systems need some way of storing the electricity. Arrays of batteries hooked together fill the need for backup power.

Homeowners with access to a public electric utility can draw on that power when there isn't enough solar power. They can also sell power back to the utility when they have an excess, although at a rate of less than they would pay for it. Each roofing system has electrical meters on the back of the panel array that connect the PV system to the grid.

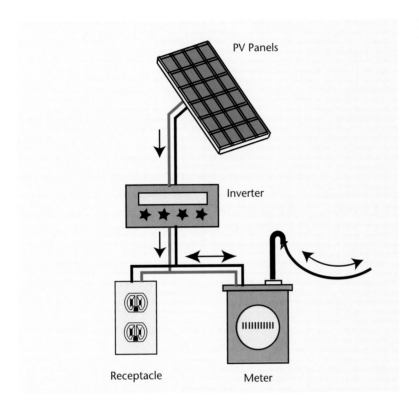

Figure 9.12 Diagram of a home photovoltaic (PV) system. PV panels on the roof convert solar energy to DC electrical current. An inverter changes it to AC, to power household circuits. The inverter interfaces with the utility's power feed in the meter, to enable the homeowner to sell excess power to the utility.

How does a PV system affect your kitchen and bath design? Solar energy varies with the time of day and time of year, so the amount of solar electricity varies. Homes equipped with PV systems should minimize their dependency on electricity by choosing appliances and fixtures that run off other energy sources, where possible. Gas-powered water heaters, clothes washers and ranges should replace their electrical counterparts. Low-voltage and energy-efficient lighting should be chosen, where feasible.

CHAPTER 10: Lighting

Lighting can spell the difference between success and failure for a kitchen or bath design. That said, lighting is one of the most exciting parts of the design process, made more so because of the new products available to designers. The part you play in the lighting design can vary, depending on how the project is set up. At the most, you may have total responsibility for the lighting in the rooms included in your design. Or you may be responsible for specifying the type and locations of the fixtures, leaving the final product selection to the client. If an architect or electrical engineer has the overall responsibility for lighting design, your role may be limited to consulting. But whatever role you play, you should know something about the basics of lighting and the particular needs of kitchens and baths.

LIGHTING BASICS

The physics of lighting are complex and beyond the scope of this book. When exploring the topic in depth, you'll run across many terms —flux, luminance, lux, footcandles and lumens—to name a few. Unless you intend on specializing in lighting design, the following should suffice for your work in kitchen and bath design.

We measure lighting intensity in **lumens (lum)**. In the SI system of units (*Système Internationale*, the metric system) one lumen is the amount of light energy that falls on a spherical surface of one square meter, produced by a single candle. The American System (AS) uses **footcandles (fc)**, where one fc is the amount of light that falls on a square foot of spherical surface at a distance of one foot from the candle. The relationship between lumens and footcandles is 1 lum = 12.57 fc.

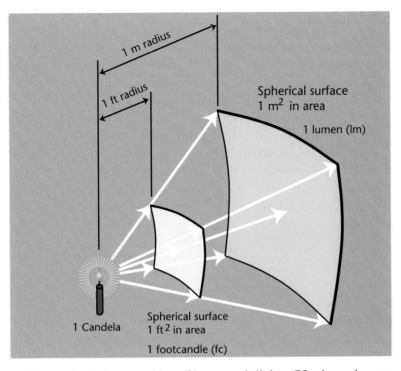

Figure 10.1 When a light source strikes a surface, we measure the amount of light striking the surface in "luminous flux." The luminous flux of one candle-power (or candela) on one square foot of spherical surface at a distance of one foot away from the source is one footcandle, or lumen. In the SI system, one lumen equals the luminous flux of one candela on a surface of one square meter, one meter away from the source.

You probably have an idea of how much light a 75w incandescent bulb delivers. However, as a designer, you should get used to comparing light output in lumens, not watts, because the wattage measures only the power consumed, not the light produced. And lamps differ in their light output per watt. A 15w compact fluorescent lamp, for example, delivers as many lumens as the 75w incandescent bulb mentioned above.

LIGHTING BY FUNCTION

A good overall goal for artificial lighting—i.e. lighting that doesn't come from the sun—is to provide enough of the right kind of light for the occupants to function within the space. That can mean anything from being able to see the chopping block when cutting up vegetables to creating a relaxing mood with the soft glow of a special lamp above a dining table. Sorted by function, there are three types of lighting: ambient, task and accent lighting.

Ambient Lighting

All rooms need some lighting to enable the occupants to get around without bumping into things. During the day, natural sunlight can provide most of this **general** or **ambient** lighting in a house if there are ample windows in the right locations. Lighting at night can come from direct or indirect sources, or a combination of these. **Direct** lighting is the light a fixture throws directly into a room or on a task surface. An example is a ceiling fixture that lights up an entire room. **Indirect** lighting reaches the room after it has bounced off another surface. For example, lamps mounted in a cove below the ceiling throw light up onto the ceiling, which bounces it down into the room.

Task Lighting

The general lighting that ambient sources disburse in a room may be adequate for some activities but fall short for others such as reading, writing, preparing meals and other focused activity. Task lighting includes light sources specifically designed to make up this shortfall. The swivel lamp on your desk is a good example. We'll see task lighting examples for kitchens and baths further on.

Accent Lighting

Stores would sell far less merchandise without displaying it in the most favorable lighting. Commercial lighting designers go to great lengths to make sure the goods are illuminated to catch the eye of shoppers. Homes can also use accent lighting to focus attention on special items, such as artwork, china or collectibles. Lighting fixtures specialized for accent lighting throw a narrow beam that highlights the object of attention without spilling into the room.

LIGHTING SOURCES

The terms "ambient," "task," and "accent" describe lighting by its intended function. Artificial lighting also varies by the way it is produced, its color, energy consumption and lamp shape and sizes. And by **"lamp,"** we mean the basic item we fit into a **fixture**, which is the assembly that includes the mounting base, or socket and features that reflect or disperse the light from the lamp. To select the right type of lighting source for a particular application you need to understand both. Your best source of information for fixtures is manufacturers' catalogs. Here are some of the standard and emerging lighting sources used in residential lighting fixtures:

Incandescent

Ever since Alexander Graham Bell invented the incandescent light bulb in the 1900s it has been the mainstay of home lighting. It hasn't changed much since the early models, either and still offers a warm, friendly color, low price and convenience. Light comes from a tungsten filament that has high resistance to electrical current. Passing an electrical current through the filament converts some of the energy into light, the rest into heat. Because of the high heat, incandescent lamps are the least efficient lighting sources. And the advantage of a low initial cost is eaten away in time, because bulbs burn out after around 750 hours of use.

Even with the drawbacks, incandescent lamps remain popular, partially because the wide variety of wattages and bulb types makes it easy to pick a lamp for almost any application. Incandescent lamps are available in both frosted and clear bulbs in a variety of shapes and designs. Here are some of the most frequently used incandescent lamp types in homes.

A lamps are the basic bulbs with standard screw-in bases that come in wattages from 25 to 150. They throw light in all directions from the bulb pretty equally and suit general illumination or task lighting if fitted into a fixture that has a reflector.

G lamps are similar to A lamps, but with bigger and rounder globes, hence the designation, "G." The shape, however, is an esthetic, rather than functional feature, intended for fixtures that do not hide the bulb, such as strip fixtures around mirrors in baths.

P lamps and **PAR lamps** have built-in reflectors to limit the light throw. A P lamp throws out a cone-shaped light pattern, whereas a PAR lamp directs its light in a cylindrical pattern, thanks to its parabolic-shaped reflector. Both types are used in spotlights and can-type fixtures. Wattages range between 50 and 150.

B lamps and **CA tipped lamps** are small bulbs for decorative uses, such as in chandeliers. B lamps are oval in shape, while CA tipped lamps are flame-shaped. Both have screw-in bases, but smaller in diameter than A lamps. Wattages range from 25 to 40.

Miniature bulbs, also used for decorative applications, are manufactured with wedge bases and bayonet bases.

Figure 10.2 Incandescent lamps come in many sizes, wattages, and configurations. Inexpensive to buy, they are also the most wasteful of electricity. A, G, PAR and R bulbs screw into standard sockets. R and PAR have reflectors built in. B and CA tipped bulbs are used in chandeliers and accent lighting. Miniature bayonet and wedge-based bulbs, similarly used, need transformers to step the voltage down to 12V.

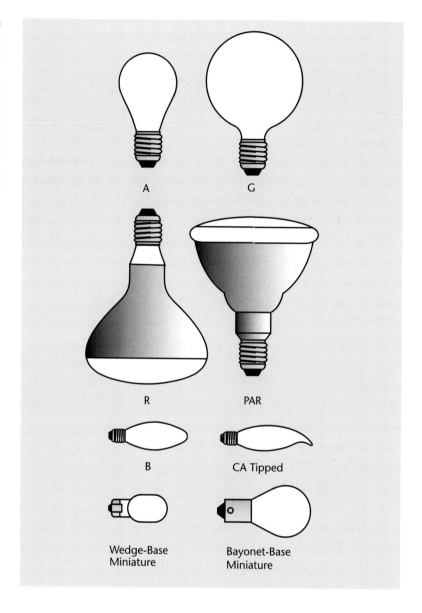

Halogen

An improved version of standard incandescent lamps, developed over the last two decades, is particularly suited to residential applications. Tungsten halogen ("halogen") lamps encase the filament inside a capsule containing halogen gas produced by iodine vapor. The gas slows filament wear through a complicated regenerative cycle and improves the efficiency of the lamp. Halogen lamps cut energy use by 30 to 50 percent, compared to long-life incandescents. Lamp life ranges between 2,000 and 3,500 hours. The light color is whiter than incandescent lamps, but not bluish enough to make food look unappetizing. Halogen lamps are available in low-voltage (12v) and standard (120v) voltages, in reflector shapes and mini-bulbs. One type of halogen lamp gets its name from the hockey puck, because of its shape. The flat profile of puck lights makes them well suited for under-cabinet applications.

Halogen lamps that run off 120v electricity become hot. If they are adjacent to cabinets finished with laminate, the heat may, in time, cause delamination. Also, avoid locating halogen lamps below a microwave oven because the heat from the lamp can cause the microwave to overheat.

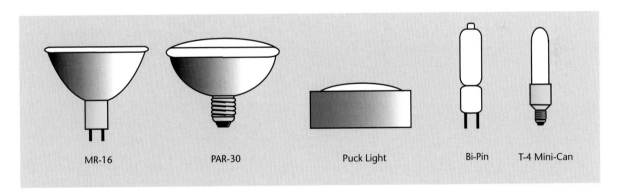

MR-16   PAR-30   Puck Light   Bi-Pin   T-4 Mini-Can

Figure 10.3 Halogen lamps offer greater efficiency than incandescent, have more precise beams and whiter color, closer to sunlight. All shown here except the PAR-30 work off 12v and need a transformer. MR and PAR lamps work well in track lights and recessed fixtures. Puck lights, bi-pins and mini cans suit under-counter lighting.

Xenon

Originally developed as brighter lights for auto headlamps and for industrial applications, xenon lamps now offer residential designers new lighting opportunities. Xenon lamps contain two electrodes in an extremely small tube filled with inert gasses. Electrical current arcs between the electrodes to yield a bright light with a color resembling sunlight. Xenon lamps have some of the qualities of halogen, but don't burn quite as hot. The color is a little warmer, but not as warm as incandescent. The real plus is the lamp life, rated at around 20,000 hours—long enough to last a typical under-cabinet installation for 50 years. Xenon lamps are miniature size with pin bases. Fixtures for under-cabinet or display case applications include strips with festoon mini-bulbs mounted at 4 or 6 inches apart (102 mm, 152 mm), as well as individual lamps that can mount at any spacing. Transformers are required to convert AC to 12v or 24v DC.

Figure 10.4 Many strip fixtures with xenon or halogen mini-bulbs are now available and are well suited for under-cabinet and accent lighting applications. The strip fixture shown uses 5w, 24v xenon mini-bulbs spaced 1 7/8 inches (48 mm) or 2 inches (51 mm) apart, in lengths from 11 inches (279 mm) up to 191 inches (4,851 mm) long.

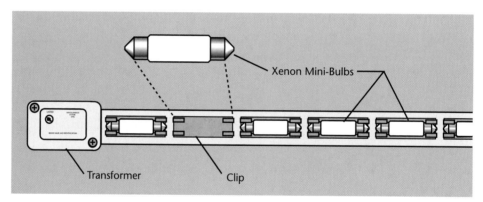

Fluorescent

Fluorescent lamps yield five times as much light as incandescent lamps for the same amount of power and last much longer. These advantages have made fluorescent lighting the first choice for commercial buildings for years. The biggest downside is that the bluish light color made people look like ghosts. So, even commercial buildings limited the use of fluorescent lighting to general lighting, never placing it above meat counters or booths in restaurants. The color ruled out fluorescent lighting for all but garages and basements of most homes. All that changed in the 1980s when newer coatings for the insides of fluorescent tubes made them yield much warmer colored light. Another change that made fluorescent bulbs acceptable in homes came around the same time, when manufacturers found ways to squeeze a long tube into a bulb that screwed into a standard household lighting fixture socket. The result was a set of **compact fluorescents** that were not only interchangeable with incandescent bulbs, but delivered a more flattering light color to skin and most foods. Today's compact fluorescents cost more, initially, than incandescents, but save in the long run because of lower operating costs and longer lifetimes.

Fluorescent lamps do not contain a resistance filament, like incandescent lamps. Instead, a heated cathode at one end of the tube produces free electrons, which are accelerated by a voltage placed across the electrodes at either end of the tube. As they accelerate, they ionize a gas vapor (mercury) in the tube, causing an arc to flash the length of the tube. The arc excites the vapor in the tube to produce light. All fluorescent lamps need ballasts to heat the cathode and run the tubes at the correct voltages. Straight-tube fluorescents have a separate ballast housed somewhere within the fixture. Compact fluorescents contain the ballast within the base. Standard magnetic-type ballasts produce an annoying flicker as well as perceptible hum and lamps coupled to them are not dimmable. The newer solid-state electronic ballasts are quieter, with less flicker and do allow dimming.

Fluorescent tubes make good candidates for side lighting of bathroom mirrors and under-cabinet lighting for kitchen countertops. But for applications in kitchens and baths, stay away from lamps in the cool-color range. Warmer colored "daylight," "deluxe cool white," "warm white," or "natural" compliment skin tones and most foods.

Figure 10.5 Today's fluorescent lamps offer better color rendition and come in a wide variety of sizes and shapes including compact fluorescent bulbs that screw into standard sockets.

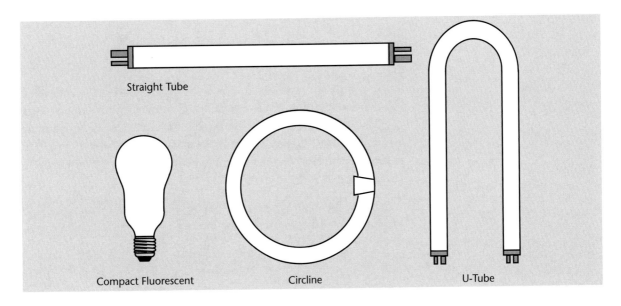

Straight Tube

Compact Fluorescent

Circline

U-Tube

THE COLOR OF LIGHT

We didn't think much about light color in the old days, when the choices were limited to incandescent or fluorescent lamps. We knew that the warm light of incandescent lamps complimented people's skin tones and enhanced foods such as meat and most vegetables. The cool light of fluorescent lamps made people look ashen, but green salads look more appetizing. But what exactly do we mean by "warm" or "cool" light?

The lighting industry uses two color indices for lighting color: *color temperature* and *color rendition*.

Color temperature is an index of how the light source, itself, looks to us, measured in degrees Kelvin (K). Warm-light sources have color temperatures less than 3000K. Light sources between 3000K and 4000K are considered neutral in color. Anything above 4000K is cool.

Color rendition is an index of how the light makes objects appear. How accurately a lighting source defines objects is measured by the **Color Rendering Index (CRI)**. The best score is 100, the CRI of sunlight.

Why do we need two indices? Because sources with the same CRI can produce different moods at different color temperatures. When specifying fluorescent lamps for home applications, you'll get the best all-around light color with tubes coated with rare-earth phosphors. Artificial light sources vary widely in their color-rendering indices. Incandescent lamps are rated at a CRI of 100—nearly equal to sunlight. Lamps with very low CRI numbers are unacceptable in home lighting. Those ghastly orange street lamps that use high-pressure sodium have a CRI of 22. Here are some rules of thumb for selecting lamps for the right color:

Task, accent and art lighting use halogen or xenon lamps. Small voltage lamps such as PAR halogen or MR 16 work better for art, because they throw their heat back away from the object.

General lighting. PAR halogen and compact fluorescents work well, but make sure the compact fluorescents have a color temperature of about 3500K (they range from 2700 to 6500K). If you use fluorescent tubes, choose lamps with a CRI over 80 and a color temperature of 3000 – 3500K.

Dining lighting. Wasteful as they are, incandescent lamps are hard to beat for the soft, warm lighting they cast on food and people's skin.

**COMPARING
LIGHTING SOURCES**

COMPARING LIGHTING SOURCES					
Type	Output, lumens	Color Temperature (°K)	Efficicacy, lum/W	Pros	Cons
Incandescent	126 (15W) – 1380 (100W) 6100 (300W)	2550 – 2800	8.4 13.8 20.3	Low initial cost. Good color. Convenient. Dimmable. Many lamp sizes & shapes.	High ultimate cost. Short life. Energy inefficient. Produces heat.
Fluorescent (straight tubes)	1350 (24") – 2900 (48")	3000	58 – 85	Efficient. Long life. Choice of light color. Distributes light evenly. Choice of lamp sizes & shapes.	Magnetic ballasts noisy, flicker and not dimmable.
Compact Fluorescent	900 – 1100	2700	40 – 60	Efficient. Long life. Choice of light color. Choice of lamp sizes & shapes.	First cost expensive, compared to incandescent.
Halogen	2500 (100W) –	2850 – 3000	25 –	Efficient. Full-spectrum white color similar to sunlight. Small shapes.	Higher first cost than incandescent. Low-voltage halogen lamps need a transformer.
Xenon (festoon mini-bulbs)	50 (5W) 120 (10W)	3000	10 12	Full-spectrum white color similar to sunlight. Small shapes work with under-counter applications.	Higher first cost than incandescent. Need transformer.

Figure 10.6 The color temperature of lamps

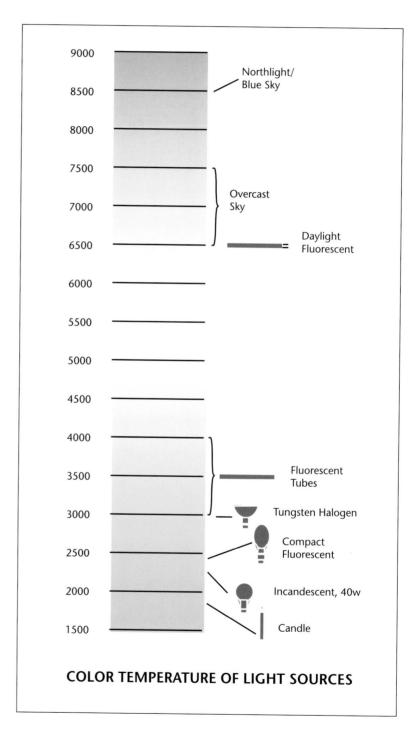

COLOR TEMPERATURE OF LIGHT SOURCES

BUILT-IN LIGHTING

Getting light to the target requires not only a lamp, but also an assembly to house the lamp and control its beam. Lamps can either be built into the structure or enclosed in manufactured fixtures (also called "luminaires"). Built-in lighting uses a site-built structure to focus or diffuse the light. Here are some typical ways to build in lighting.

Under Cabinets. Mount lamps under wall cabinets near the front edge, so they throw light directly on the countertop, where it is most needed for food preparation. Lamps suited for this include fluorescent tubes, halogen or xenon puck lights and xenon strips.

Above Cabinets. The same types of lamps mounted on top of wall cabinets can bathe the ceiling in light for ambient lighting.

Coves and Valances. Horizontal baffles running around the room below the ceiling can hide strip lighting (usually fluorescent tubes), for soft, ambient room lighting. A light cove directs light up onto the ceiling, which reflects it back down in a diffuse pattern. Cove lighting works best when the ceiling is painted flat white or off-white. A valance has an open bottom as well as top to allow the light to both wash the ceiling and wall below.

Figure 10.7 Lighting can be built into the structure or cabinetry to illuminate any selected surface and to disperse light directly or indirectly. Direct light, such as shown in an under-cabinet application, throws focused illumination on areas where higher levels are necessary for tasks such as food preparation. Bouncing light off walls and ceilings creates a softer, less intense level for ambient lighting.

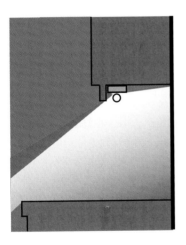

DIRECT, UNDER-CABINET

INDIRECT, COVE LIGHT

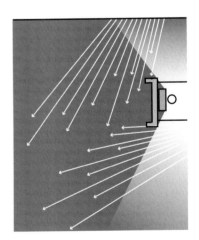

INDIRECT, WALL WASHER

LIGHTING FIXTURES

You'll find an amazing variety of manufactured lighting fixtures. In time your office shelves will probably be overloaded with lighting catalogs, from which you can select fixtures of almost any type or style. Here's a rundown of the basic types and their design implications:

Recessed Ceiling Fixtures

Mounting a fixture into, rather than onto the ceiling hides the fixture. The effect is a spot of light coming through a hole in the ceiling. You can choose between recessed fixtures that hold the lamp in a fixed position or units with the lamp mounted in an "eyeball" that swivels. Some fixtures come with reflectors built in (Alzak type) and require an A lamp, either incandescent or halogen. Others have corrugated baffles painted white or black. White baffles direct more light downward but are harsher to look at.

Recessed fixtures generally throw a cone-shaped beam to illuminate a limited area. A single recessed fixture in the center of a room wouldn't light up the whole room, as would a pendant or surface-mounted one that delivered light in all directions. Thus, recessed fixtures are best installed in multiples, spaced 24 to 42 inches (610 mm to 1,067 mm) apart. To determine the best spacing for a particular fixture, get the angle of the beam spread from the manufacturer's specs, then position fixtures so that the beams overlap at the intended target. For example, if you are using recessed fixtures to light up a countertop, you want the beams to overlap at a height of 36 inches (914 mm).

One more tip: recessed fixtures give off a lot of heat. The NEC requires a separation of at least 1/2 inch (13 mm) between the fixture and any combustible material and a separation of 3 inches (76 mm) from any insulation, unless a type "IC" housing is specified, which may abut combustibles and insulation.

Surface-Mounted Ceiling Fixtures

Mounting the light source on, rather than in, the ceiling enables it to throw light in all directions, an asset when designing ambient lighting. You will get a better effect by using several fixtures located around the edge of a room than a single one in the center of the room. Surface fixtures are shaped as drums, cones, squares and spheres, in single or multiple configurations. Choice of lamps ranges between incandescent, halogen and compact fluorescent. Manufacturers' specifications state the maximum wattage permitted to avoid fire hazard.

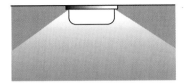

CEILING FIXTURE

Suspended Fixtures

By hanging a fixture by a chain from the ceiling, we can bring the light source down into the room for more intimacy, particularly in dining areas. There are two types of suspended fixtures, though the distinctions often get blurred. **Chandeliers** descended from the elaborate assemblies of candles that hung from castle ceilings. Today's versions retain some of the effect with multiple flame-shaped or other mini-bulbs that mimic the light of candles. **Pendants** are a less formal modern adaptation of the idea, which hold one or more lamps. You can choose pendants that direct light evenly in all directions, focus it up or down, or only down. Wiring the fixture to a dimmer switch enables the diners to adjust the lighting level to suit the mood of the meal.

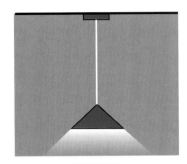

PENDANT

Track Lights

Lighting fixtures that slide in tracks enable homeowners to add or reposition the fixtures as needed. They offer even greater flexibility because the fixtures swivel and rotate. Because of their adjustability, track lights can wash walls, illuminate countertops, or artwork. The tracks mount on the ceiling or, if the ceiling is high enough, hang from legs. Individual lamps insert into the track and make contact with two conductors, mounted in parallel inside the track. Lamp housings could be cans, with or without baffles and reflectors, much the same as for recessed fixtures. Similarly, lamp types vary, though many favor lamps with built-in reflectors (PAR or MR).

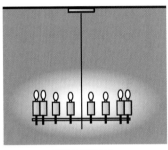

CHANDELIER

Wall-Mounted Fixtures

After the fixtures, cabinets and mirrors are located in the design, kitchens and baths tend to have little free wall area for wall-mounted lighting fixtures. Still, there may be areas where a wall-mounted fixture makes sense. **Sconces** are single-bulb fixtures that throw light out, up, down, or a combination of these, based on the design of the diffuser lens, baffle, or reflector housing. They can mount on the wall surface or be recessed. Use the manufacturer's recommendations for the appropriate lamp type.

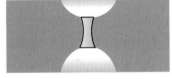

SCONCE

Another type of wall-mounted fixture is **strip lighting**, usually an array of individual lamps mounted into a strip base or a single fluorescent tube with a diffuser lens. Multiple-lamp strips take A, G, or mini lamps. Tube strips take fluorescent lamps of various lengths, from 16 to 48 inches (406 mm to 1,219 mm). Strip lights are well-suited to baths, as we'll see further on.

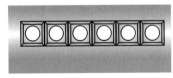

STRIP FIXTURE

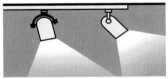

TRACK LIGHTS

Figure 10.8 Lighting fixtures are available in an infinite variety and can be suspended or surface-mounted on ceilings, walls and cabinetry. Track lighting enables the user to adjust the location and direction of a beam.

LIGHTING KITCHENS

Good lighting in the kitchen is probably harder than any other space in the house. First, all work areas need adequate task light of the right color and intensity. The room also needs ambient light for general illumination. If a dining area is part of the kitchen, it should be lit with a source that fosters enjoyment of the meal. Can all these goals be met? The answer is yes, with sensitive lighting strategies.

Lighting Work Areas

Food preparation is a demanding task, so the goal of task lighting is to put the light on the work surfaces, most of which are on countertops around the periphery of the room. In the quest for economy, many mass-produced houses light the entire kitchen with a single fixture in the center of the ceiling, with the worst possible results, guaranteed to cast the cook's shadow on any work surface not directly under the fixture. A much better approach is to locate fixtures at the ceiling just in front of the wall cabinets or under the wall cabinets. Ranges can be lit with lights built into range hoods. If you are designing a custom hood, it too should contain a fixture. For downdraft ventilating ranges, mount a recessed or surface-mounted fixture above the range.

The best location for countertop lighting is below the wall cabinets, with the fixtures mounted near the front edge. Lamps mounted here throw their light directly on the work surface, with no objects intervening to cast a shadow. Fluorescent lamps mounted end-to-end work well, if the lamps have a color temperature above 3500K. Another solution is to mount individual halogen or xenon puck lights 12 inches (305 mm) apart. You can also use xenon strip fixtures, which contain mini xenon bulbs mounted 4 inches (102 mm) apart.

If you choose to light the countertop from the ceiling, locate the fixtures close enough to the wall so that they won't cast the user's shadow on the countertop, but with enough clearance for the doors of the wall cabinets to open. Fixtures can be recessed or surface-mounted on the ceiling or recessed into an overhanging soffit. Can lights and spots work well at the ceiling level and if mounted in tracks, enable the homeowner to adjust their location and focus.

Figure 10.9 Achieve balanced illumination by combining under-cabinet fixtures for direct lighting on the work surfaces with ambient lighting from an omni-directional ceiling fixture.

Figure 10.10 The same kitchen shown in Figure 10.9 with direct lighting from lamps recessed in an overhanging soffit.

Figure 10.11 Yet another way to get direct lighting on the work surface is to install track lighting in front of the cabinets. An added plus is the lighting can be adjusted, as needed. This approach, however, only works if the ceiling is high enough to ensure that the cabinet doors swing clear of the lamps when open.

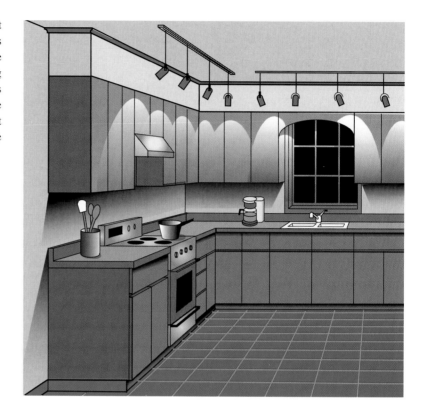

The Rest of the Kitchen

Successful ambient lighting provides evenly distributed light that doesn't cause glare or discomfort. The single fixture in the center of the ceiling, mentioned earlier, may satisfy the first need, but not the second, since anyone sitting in the room can't look up at the ceiling without squinting. If a single fixture is the only choice for ambient lighting, one that bounces light off the ceiling gives a better result. Better still is to use more than a single source, such as strips or individual fixtures mounted on the tops of the wall cabinets, as shown in Figure 10.12. With experience, you'll most likely discover other ways to achieve good general lighting.

If a dining area is included as part of the kitchen—on an island or separate table—it should be lit with a source that provides both enough light to see the food and create the mood to want to eat it. But these needs are not the same for every meal. The breakfast eaten quickly on a dark morning needs a different quality light than a fancy dinner intended to be enjoyed in a relaxed atmosphere. An oft-chosen answer to this is a pendant centered over the dining surface. Another possibility is surface-mounted or recessed cans. If there is a wall surface, a sconce might work. In any case, the fixture should be connected to a dimmer switch, so that the lighting level can be adjusted to suit the mood. Figure 10.12 shows how combining a pendant at the dining area with above cabinet lighting provides good ambient lighting for the room (actually for relaxed dining, the cabinet lights can be turned off, allowing the dining surface to be the focus).

Figure 10.12 A kitchen with a dining area needs a light source there. In this example, a pendant illuminates the table, with lighting for food preparation provided by under-cabinet lighting. Strip fixtures above the cabinets supply ambient lighting.

Accent Lighting

As homeowners regard kitchens as living space, as well as a place to prepare food, they increasingly want to display art, china and collectibles in the kitchen. Wall-mounted art can best be lit with adjustable fixtures mounted on the ceiling at a distance of 24 to 30 inches (610 mm to 762 mm) out from the wall, as shown in Figure 10.13. Another solution is recessed ceiling fixtures, as shown in Figure 10.14. Eyeball type fixtures that rotate in their housing allow the direction of the light to be adjusted.

Figure 10.13 Guidelines for using track lighting to illuminate objects on a wall, the wall itself, or any vertical surface. Courtesy of the American Lighting Association.

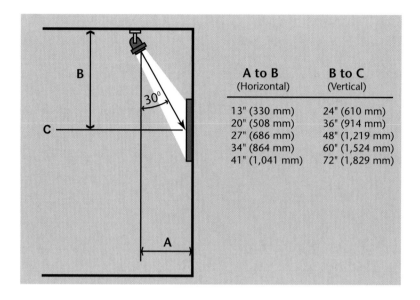

A to B (Horizontal)	B to C (Vertical)
13" (330 mm)	24" (610 mm)
20" (508 mm)	36" (914 mm)
27" (686 mm)	48" (1,219 mm)
34" (864 mm)	60" (1,524 mm)
41" (1,041 mm)	72" (1,829 mm)

Figure 10.14 Guidelines for using recessed fixtures for accent lighting. Matching the lamp type correctly with the vertical and horizontal distances shown will ensure levels of 20 to 60fc at the center of the beam. Courtesy of the American Lighting Association.

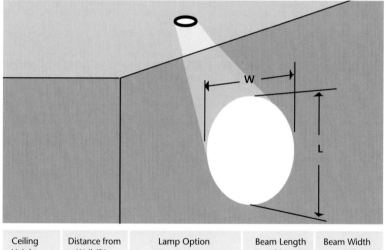

Ceiling Height	Distance from Wall (D)	Lamp Option	Beam Length (L)	Beam Width (W)
8' (2,438 mm)	2' (610 mm)	50W PAR-36 WFL (12V)	5' (1,524 mm)	2'-6" (762 mm)
		50W MR-16 FL (12V)	8' (2,438 mm)	3' (914 mm)
		75W R-30 SP	4'-6"(1,372 mm)	2' (610 mm)
		75W R-30 FL	to floor	7' (2,134 mm)
10' (3,048 mm)	3' (914 mm)	75W PAR-38 FL	5'-6" (1,676 mm)	2' (610 mm)
		25W PAR-36 NSP (12V)	2' (610 mm)	1' (304 mm)
		50W MR-16 NSP (12V)	2' (610 mm)	1'-6" (457 mm)
		50W MR-16 NFL (12V)	5'-6" (1,676 mm)	3' (914 mm)
		75W PAR-38 SP	3' (914 mm)	1'-6" (457 mm)

For china and other items displayed behind glass doors, you'll get a good effect with small low-voltage strip lighting, such as xenon strips, mounted atop the cabinet just behind the door.

LIGHTING BATHS

The 5 foot x 7 foot (1,524 mm x 2,134 mm) bath that was the standard in production housing of past decades often made do with a single ceiling fixture for ambient lighting and possibly another fixture above the lav for task lighting. As baths grow in size and amenity, they require more sensitive lighting. For one thing, a larger bath may not be just *one* room, but a room with several sub-rooms to enclose tubs, showers or toilets—each needing a source of light. So the goal, once again, is to deliver lighting where it is needed.

Vanities and Lavs

The space between the lav and the wall is one of the most critical but least forgiving areas for bathroom lighting. People must be able to see the lav or vanity as well as themselves in the mirror above. To do this, the fixture must illuminate the person's face. The simplest solution is a fixture above the mirror. This is also the worst, since the fixture throws light downward onto the person's face, causing shadows below the eyebrows, nose and chin—just what you don't want when shaving or putting on makeup. A much better approach is to locate sconces or—better—strip lighting at the sides of the mirror, where they can light the face more evenly. Two fluorescent tubes mounted behind a valance above the mirror can also work by bouncing light off the wall before it hits the person's face. But the wall must be white or near-white and even then might not be as effective as side-mounted fixtures.

Figure 10.15 The best way to ensure even light on the face of a person standing before a mirror is to mount the light source at the side of the mirror. Strip fixtures spread a more evenly distributed beam than do fixtures with a single bulb. In small bathrooms, additional fixtures, such as the recessed ceiling lamps shown, may not be needed. However, make sure the shower gets enough light from the room or is equipped with its own light source.

147

Figure 10.16 Task lighting at the vanity can also come from a strip fixture mounted behind a valance (two 40w T8 bulbs). As in the example in Figure 10.15, make sure the rest of the room is adequately lit.

Showers, Tubs and Toilets

A pleasing and economical way to illuminate the small sub-spaces of a bathroom is directly through their walls. Glass blocks or obscure (patterned) glass in these walls enable the enclosed space to borrow light from the main space. If this isn't feasible, these spaces can usually be well lit with a single ceiling fixture, recessed or surface mounted. Many exhaust fans contain a lamp. If your design includes a separate lighting fixture over a wet area, make sure it is a water-resisting type.

Your client may want a heat lamp in the bath. If you include one, locate it in the ceiling above an open area with enough room for the person standing below it to move about. Because heat lamps consume a lot of electricity, they should always be switched separately from other fixtures. The NKBA recommends heat lamps be wired to a separate circuit and connected to a timer switch.

Ambient Lighting

If you provide adequate light at the mirror and bathing areas you may not need any other lighting in a bath. If you do, consider a recessed ceiling fixture or two, or wall sconces.

Kitchen & Bath Systems

A

AC: (see "Alternating Current").

Accent Lighting: Lighting that emphasizes displayed items, such as artwork or china cupboards.

Active Solar Heating: Collecting the sun's heat into a liquid medium or air, then circulating the medium into heat exchangers inside the house to yield usable heat.

AFUE: Annual Fuel Utilization Efficiency, a measure of the efficiency of heating devices, which is the percentage of fuel converted to space heat.

Air Chamber: A device containing a pocket of air which, when connected in the water piping near a fixture, expands and contracts to prevent the sudden jolt called water hammer.

Air Gap: *1.* The negative pressure that can result when a hand-held shower faucet or sink sprayer is dropped into a sink or tub. If negative pressure exists, wastewater can be siphoned out into the supply system. Newer products have backflow protection or a vacuum breaker (vertical spray bidet) to prevent the problem. *2.* A fitting on the high end of the waste hose loop to prevent siphoning.

Alternating Current (AC): The type of current used in household wiring. The current changes polarity, or alternates, continually from positive to negative and back again at the rate of 60 times a second.

Alzak: A type of reflector in recessed lighting fixtures, in silver or gold color.

Ambient Lighting: General lighting diffused within an entire room.

Ambient: The environment surrounding us. In the context of buildings, the environmental conditions in the room.

Amperes, Amps: Unit of electrical current. The current in amps equals the power in watts divided by the voltage in volts.

Anthracite: A hard coal used for home heating.

Aquifer: A strata in the ground that contains water.

Armored (BX) Cable: Electrical wires encased in a flexible metal sheathing.

AWG: American Wire Gauge, a system for classifying wire by size.

B

Backdrafting: Sucking air out of combustion appliances caused by depressurizing the home with devices that exhaust air to the outside, without replacing it with fresh air.

Ballast: A device that controls the current in a fluorescent lamp.

Bituminous: A soft coal used primarily to generate electricity and make coke for the steel industry.

Black Wire: A "hot" wire in a two- or three-conductor cable.

Boiler: The central heating device in a hydronic or steam heating system.

Btu: British Thermal Unit, a measurement of heat quantity in countries using the British system. One Btu is the amount of heat energy required to raise the temperature of one pound of water by one degree Fahrenheit.

Bulkhead: A "soffit" in Canadian usage. The under surface of a lowered portion of the ceiling.

Btuh: British Thermal Units per Hour (see "Btu").

Bus: A flat bar inside an electrical power panel into which branch circuit breakers are plugged.

Butane: A type of natural gas.

C

Cable: *1.* A bundle of electrical conductors, or wires, containing one or more insulated hot wires, an insulated neutral or white wire and a bare or ground wire. *2.* Two or more wires bundled inside a protective sheathing of plastic or metal.

Chandelier: A lighting fixture hung from the ceiling containing several small lamps.

Chlorinated Polyvinyl Chloride: An improved version of PVC, suitable for both hot and cold domestic water supply piping.

Chlorine: A chemical of the trihalomethane group that is used to kill microorganisms in drinking water, but toxic in excessive concentrations.

Circuit Breaker: A protective switch that automatically switches off, or trips, the power to a circuit in the event of an overload or short in the circuit.

CO: Carbon monoxide, a deadly gas that is colorless, odorless and tasteless.

Color Rendering Index (CRI): A measurement of how accurately a lighting source defines objects. The best score is 100, the CRI of sunlight.

Color Rendition: An index of how the light makes objects appear.

Color Temperature: An index of how the light source, itself, looks to us, measured in degrees Kelvin (K).

Combustion Air: Air required for burning by appliances containing a flame.

Comfort Zone: The region of a graph depicting comfort felt by people exposed to various temperatures, humidity levels and air movement

Compact Fluorescent (CFL): A type of fluorescent lamp with the fluorescent tube coiled into a compact shape in a size similar to an incandescent bulb.

Condensing Boilers: A type of boiler that achieves efficiencies of up to 95% by incorporating a second heat exchanger that recoups some of the heat from the hot exhaust gasses to pre-heat the water in the boiler system.

Conduction: The flow of heat energy through a material. Heat flows from the warmer to cooler side of the material.

Conduit: As used in electricity, a metal or plastic tube containing electrical cables.

Contrast: The difference in brightness between surfaces in the field of view.

Convection: The transmission of heat through a liquid or gas. The cooler feeling you experience in front of a fan in summer is due to convective air movement over your skin.

Cord: The quantity of wood that can be stacked in a volume measuring 4 feet x 4 feet x 8 feet

Counterflow Furnace: (see "Downflow Furnace").

CPVC: (see "Chlorinated Polyvinyl Chloride").

Crawl Space: An open space below the first floor and ground, usually high enough to crawl through.

Cross-Linked Polyethylene (PEX): A flexible plastic piping, made from molecules cross linked to form a durable material, and used for domestic hot and cold water supply and radiant heating piping.

D

Daylighting: Using light from the sun to illuminate the interior of a building.

DC: Direct current, commonly supplied by batteries and photovoltaic generating systems.

Dewpoint Temperature: The temperature at which moisture begins to form on a slick surface indicating 100% saturation. The temperature at which the wet bulb and dry bulb temperatures are the same.

Dielectric Union: A pipe fitting that keeps two pipes of dissimilar metals from direct contact with each other to prevent corrosion through electrolytic action.

Diffuser: In heating and cooling systems, a grill, or register, in a floor or wall that delivers conditioned air to the room. In lighting, a diffuser is a transparent or translucent lens that encloses the lamp.

Direct Current (DC): Steady-state current in which the positive and negative wires retain the same polarity. Batteries and PV collectors supply DC current.

Direct Gain: A method of passive solar heating by collecting the sun's heat through windows.

Direct-Vent Heater: An all-in-one heating device that draws combustion air into the fire chamber through a vent in the wall and exhaust the burnt gasses back out through another, concentric vent.

Disposer: A device mounted below the drain of a sink to grind food solid wastes into a slurry that can pass through the drain piping.

Downflow Furnace: A forced-air furnace that delivers heated air below the unit.

Dry Bulb Temperature: The ambient (surrounding) temperature taken with a thermometer.

Drywall: Gypsum-based plaster encased between two layers of facing paper, used for interior wall surfaces as a substrate for paint, wallpaper, or tile finishes.

Duplex Receptacle: A common type of receptacle that accepts two plugs.

E

EER: Energy Efficiency Rating, a standard for rating the energy efficiency of an appliance. The higher the EER number, the more efficient the appliance.

Efficacy: The energy efficiency of a lighting source, or lighting output per watt of power in lumens per watt (LPW).

El: L-shaped pipe fittings for making 90° turns.

Elbow: (see "El").

Electrical metallic tubing (EMT): A thin-walled, galvanized-steel conduit used to protect wires from damage.

Electrolytic Action: Corrosion that results from two dissimilar metals in contact with each other in the presence of an electrolyte, such as water, which contains a small amount of acid.

Energy Star: A label by the Environmental Protection Agency that rates the efficiency of energy-consuming appliances.

Envelope: The outermost parts of a building that separate the interior environment from the outside weather, usually the walls and roof.

EPDM: Ethylene propylene diene monomer, a synthetic membrane material used for roofing flat, or nearly flat, surfaces.

Evaporative Cooling: Cooling the air by blowing it through water, which then evaporates, removing heat from the air.

F

Fintube: A type of diffuser that transfers heat from a pipe to the room via a series of fins attached to the pipe.

Fitting: A device that connects lengths of pipe, or a pipe to a fixture or appliance.

Fixture (lighting): The assembly that includes the mounting base, or socket and any features that reflect or disperse the light from a lamp fitted into the fixture.

Fixture, electrical: Any device permanently, or "hard-wired," to the home wiring system.

Fixture, lighting: Any light-producing device permanently, or "hard-wired," to the home wiring system.

Fixture, plumbing: A sink or lavatory (these terms used interchangeably in this book), toilet, bathtub, spa, shower and bidet.

Fluorescent: Lighting produced by arcing an electrical current between electrodes at opposite ends of a gas-filled tube.

Footcandle (fc): A measurement in the American System (AS) for the amount of light that falls on a surface. One footcandle is the amount of light that falls on a surface one foot square, placed one foot from the source. A footcandle of illumination is a lumen of light distributed over a 1-square-foot (0.09-square-meter) area.

Foundation: The below-grade portion of the structure between the footing and main level.

Furring: Thin strips installed to a wall or ceiling surface to create a substrate for a finish material (also called "strapping").

Fuse: A safety device that protects a device or circuit from overload or a short. The mechanism is a low-conductor metal that snaps in two when the fuse blows, making replacement necessary. For this reason, fuses in household circuits have been replaced by circuit breakers.

G

Gauge: The diameter of wire. The smaller the gauge, the larger is the diameter.

Galvanized: Metal coated with zinc to resist corrosion.

GCHP: Ground-coupled heat pump, a device that uses the warmth or coolness of the ground to heat or cool a house.

GFCI: Ground Fault Circuit Interrupter. A safety circuit breaker required by the National Electrical Code for switches and receptacles in areas subject to dampness, such as kitchens and bathrooms.

Glare: Unwanted brightness that annoys, distracts, or reduces visibility.

Ground Wire: A wire that carries current into the earth to protect people from electrocution.

H

Halogen: A variation of incandescent lighting whereby the filament is encased inside a capsule containing halogen gas, produced by iodine vapor.

Hard Water: Water that contains a high level of dissolved minerals.

Hard-Wired: A permanent electrical connection for an appliance or device (as opposed to a cord with a plug).

Heat Exchanger: A means to exhaust hot air while bringing in fresh air, in which the heat transfer is indirect, thus saving energy.

Heat pump water heater (HPWH): A heat pump adapted to heat water for domestic use.

Heat Pump: A refrigeration device that can reverse the cooling cycle to produce useful heat.

Heating Element: The cylinder inside a water heater that transfers heat to the water in the tank.

Home Run: In connection with electrical or plumbing systems, a direct route between the supply source and the point of use.

HPWH: (see "Heat Pump Water Heater").

HSPF: Heating seasonal performance factor, a standard for rating the efficiency of heating equipment, which equals the total annual heating output in Btu divided by the total electrical output in watt-hours during the heating season.

HVAC: Heating, Ventilating and Air Conditioning.

Hydronic: A type of space-heating system that uses heated water as the medium.

I

Incandescent: Lighting produced when an electrical current runs through a poor conductor, such as a tungsten carbide filament in an incandescent bulb.

Inverter: A device that changes DC current to AC.

J

Junction Box: A metal or plastic box that serves as a terminus for wiring in walls or ceilings.

K

Kilowatt-hours (kWh): A measurement of power consumption over time. One kWh is the power consumed by a 1000w device operating for one hour.

Kilowatts (kW): One thousand watts.

kPa: Kilo-Pascals, a unit of pressure in the metric system (1 kPa = 6.896 psi).

L

Lamp: An interchangeable bulb or tube that constitutes the lighting source in a fixture.

Lavatory, Lav: A sink or washbasin used for personal hygiene in a bathroom.

Lens: (see "Diffuser").

Load Avoidance: Minimizing the amount of heating or cooling that must be done by mechanical equipment.

Low-E: Low emissivity. A microscopically thin, metallic coating on glass that controls the amount of solar heat that the glass transfers by radiation.

LP Gas: Liquid propane (see "Propane").

Lumen: The amount of light, measured at the lighting source.

Luminaire: (see "fixture").

Lux: A measurement in the International System (SI) for the amount of light that falls on a surface. One lux is the amount of light that falls on one square meter placed one meter from the source.

M

Manifold: In plumbing, a pipe with several take-off points to distribute water to several pipes.

N

Nitrates: By-products of fertilizer that can leach into ground water and contaminate the aquifers that supply both public and private-source drinking water.

Nonmetallic sheathed cable: (see "Romex").

O

Oakum: Hemp rope impregnated with a bituminous compound used as a back stop for molten lead in lead and oakum joints for cast iron pipe.

Ohm: The unit of measurement of electrical resistance. The resistance of an electrical device equals the line voltage divided by the rated amperage of the device.

Ohm's Law: The relationship between volts, amps and resistance (ohms): Amps = volts/ohms.

Outgassing: The slow release of chemical gasses contained within building materials to the ambient air, such as formaldehyde in particleboard.

Overload: Demand beyond the safe carrying capacity of electrical cables and circuits.

P

Panel: (see "Service Panel").

Passive Solar Heating: Using the sun's energy to heat a house with minimal dependence on mechanical devices.

PE: (see "Polyethylene Piping").

Pendant: A lighting fixture, containing one or more lamps and hung from the ceiling.

PEX: (see "Cross-Linked Polyethylene").

Photovoltaic (PV): Electricity directly converted from solar energy. The word derives from "photo" (light) and "voltaic" (electricity).

Plywood: A panel product made by cross-laminating alternate thin layers of wood.

Poly, Polyethylene: A type of plastic with many uses in construction, one of which is for vapor barriers in walls, ceilings, and roofs and under slabs.

Polybutylene: A flexible gray or black piping used for domestic hot and cold water supply.

Polyethylene (PE) Piping: A black-colored plastic pipe used for cold-water supply and underground water supply lines.

Polyvinyl Chloride (PVC): A white, semi-rigid, plastic material whose many uses in the house include cold water piping.

Potable: Water sufficiently free from impurities to allow it to be drunk without posing a hazard to health.

Propane: A type of gas delivered to home storage tanks by trucks.

psi: Pounds per square inch, a unit of pressure in the English system (1 psi = 0.1450 kPa).

P-Trap: (see "Trap").

PVC: (see "Polyvinyl Chloride").

R

Raceway: An enclosure for electrical wires, typically mounted on interior surfaces.

Radiation: The emission of energy from an object. Heat waves from the object radiate to cooler objects. Like radio waves, this form of energy passes through air without heating it; only becoming heat after it strikes and is absorbed by a dense material.

Red Wire: A "hot" wire in a three-conductor cable.

Reducer: A pipe fitting that joins two pipes of different diameters.

Register: (see "Diffuser").

Relative Humidity: The percent of moisture in the air compared to the amount of moisture the air could contain.

Return air plenum: A duct between the supply diffusers in rooms and the furnace of a forced-air heating system.

Revent: A separate vent branch connecting the drain line from a fixture or group of fixtures to the outdoors or to the main stack/vent in the house.

Romex: A type of electrical cable containing a single, hot wire encased in black plastic, a white-encased neutral wire and a bare ground wire—all wrapped inside a plastic sheath.

R-Value: A measure of resistance to the passage of heat through a material by conductance, in British Thermal Units per Hour (Btuh). Used to rate the heat resisting ability of building insulation, the higher the R-value, the more effective the insulation.

S

Sconce: A lighting fixture mounted to the wall.

SEER: Seasonal Energy Efficiency Rating: energy efficiency rating (SEER). A standard for rating the annual energy efficiency of appliances that considers the effects of climate. The higher the EER, the more efficient the appliance.

158

Kitchen & Bath Systems

Septic System: An on-site system for disposing of household sewage, consisting of a tank that partially digests the waste and a drain field that distributes the liquid into the soil.

Service Panel: The metal box that is the distribution point for household electricity. It contains the main breaker and branch circuit breakers.

Sewage: Waste containing animal or vegetable matter in suspension or solution.

Short Circuit: A fault that occurs when a bare wire contacts another bare wire carrying electricity.

Soffit: The under surface of a lowered portion of the ceiling. A "bulkhead" in Canada.

Soft Water: Water that contains a low level of dissolved minerals.

Solder: An alloy of soft metals that melt to fuse a connection between metal pipe and a fitting. Lead, the traditional base for solder is no longer acceptable in household water piping, having been replaced by silver-tin alloy.

Spa: A vessel intended for soaking in heated water.

Stack Effect: The tendency for warm air to rise in a space.

S-Trap: (see "Trap").

Sunspace: A method of passive solar heating by collecting the sun's heat into a south-facing room that can be opened or closed to the rest of the house.

Supply Plenum: The duct in a forced-air heating or air conditioning system that supplies the heated or cooled air to diffusers in the rooms.

T

Task Lighting: Lighting focused on an work area.

Tee: A pipe fitting shaped like the letter "T" with three outlets.

Thermal Break: An insulating gasket placed between the inside and outside portions of a metal window or door frame to stem heat loss and minimize condensation.

THM: (see "Trihalomethanes").

Trap: A section of pipe curved to retain water and make a seal in the line below a fixture. P-traps are shaped like the letter P, while S-traps (no longer allowed) are shaped like the letter S.

Trihalomethanes (THM): A group of chemicals toxic in excessive concentrations. These are known to cause cancer in laboratory animals.

U

Ultraviolet: An invisible portion of the light spectrum that fades fabrics.

Upflow Furnace: A forced-air furnace that delivers heated air above the unit.

V

Veiling Reflection: A kind of glare that comes from a shiny surface, such as a glass table.

VOCs: Volatile organic compounds. Toxic substances contained in paints, solvents and cleaners derived from petrochemicals.

Volatile Organic Compounds: (see "VOCs").

Voltage, Volts: Voltage is the electrical force, or pressure that pushes the current over the conductors. Volts are the measurement units

W

Wallboard: (see "Drywall").

Water Hammer: The jolt in a water pipe that occurs when the water is suddenly shut off (see "Air Chamber").

Wattage, Watts: The unit of measurement for electrical power. The power in watts equals the voltage times the amperage.

Wet Bulb Temperature: The lowest temperature level of the air that can be reached by cooling the air by evaporation.

Whirlpool: A bathing fixture equipped with jets around the bottom to circulate warm water under the pressure of a pump.

White Wire: The neutral wire in a cable.

Wye: Y-shaped pipe fittings with an in-line inlet and outlet, and a second outlet that branches off at an angle.

X

Xenon: Lighting produced by current arcing between two electrodes in an extremely small tube filled with inert gasses.

CODE DEVELOPER ASSOCIATIONS

International Association of Plumbing & Mechanical Officials (IAPMO)
5001 E. Philadelphia Street
Ontario, CA 91761
Phone 909-472-4100 • iapmo.org

International Code Council, Inc. (ICC)
5203 Leesburg Pike, Suite 600,
Falls Church, VA 22041-3401
Phone 703-931-4533 • iccsafe.org

National Fire Protection Association (NFPA)
Batterymarch Park, P.O. Box 9101,
Quincy, MA 02269-9101
Phone 617-770-3000 • nfpa.org

National Research Council of Canada
1200 Montreal Road, Building M-58, Ottawa,
Ontario, Canada K1A
Phone 613-993-9101 • nrc.ca

TRADE ASSOCIATIONS

American National Standards Institute (ANSI)
1430 Broadway, New York, NY 10018
Phone 212-642-4980 • ansi.org

American Society for Testing and Materials (ASTM)
100 Barr Harbor Drive,
West Conshohocken, PA 19428-2959
Phone 610-832-9585 • astm.org

The Association of Pool & Spa Professionals (APSP)
2111 Eisenhower Avenue, Alexandria, VA 22314
Phone 703-838-0083 • theapsp.org

National Association of Home Builders (NAHB)
1201 15th Street, NW, Washington, DC 20005
Phone 800-368-5242 • nahb.org

National Association of the Remodeling Industry (NARI)
1901 No. Moore St., Suite 808, Arlington, VA 22209
Phone 800-611-6274 • nari.org

National Electrical Manufacturing Association (NEMA)
780 Lee Street, Suite 200, Des Plaines, IL 60016
Phone 800-611-6274 • nema.org

National Kitchen & Bath Association (NKBA)
687 Willow Grove Street, Hackettstown, NJ 07840
Phone 908-852-0033 • nkba.org

Sheet Metal and Air Conditioning Contractors' National Association (SMACNA)
4201 Lafayette Center Drive,
Chantilly, VA 21151-1209
Phone 703-803-2980 • smacna.org

Underwriters Laboratories, Inc. (UL)
333 Pfingsten Road,
Northbrook, IL 60062-2096
Phone 847-272-8800 • ul.com

GAMA – An Association of Appliance & Equipment Manufacturers
2107 Wilson Blvd., Suite 600, Arlington, VA 22201
Phone 703-525-7060 • gamanet.org

INDEX